Cocktail Time! covers everything, from classic drinks (and variations on them) like martinis, negronis, and hot toddies to my own original concoctions such as the Feigtini and various holiday-themed cocktails, as well as recipes from some of my film and TV industry friends, such as the Charlize Theron Gibson, the Very Cherry Kerry (Washington), the (Angela) Kinsey Gin Fizz, Henry (Golding)'s Honey Plum G&T, and the Five (Michelle) Yeoh-Larm Fire.

Cocktail Time! is my love letter to the aesthetics and culture around cocktails. I guarantee it's going to make you want to up your party-throwing game—or at least your home bar situation. And it's what I like to think is an immensely fun and readable window into one guy's friendly obsession. Or at least I hope that's what *you* will think! Buy this book and find out!

COCKTAIL TIME!

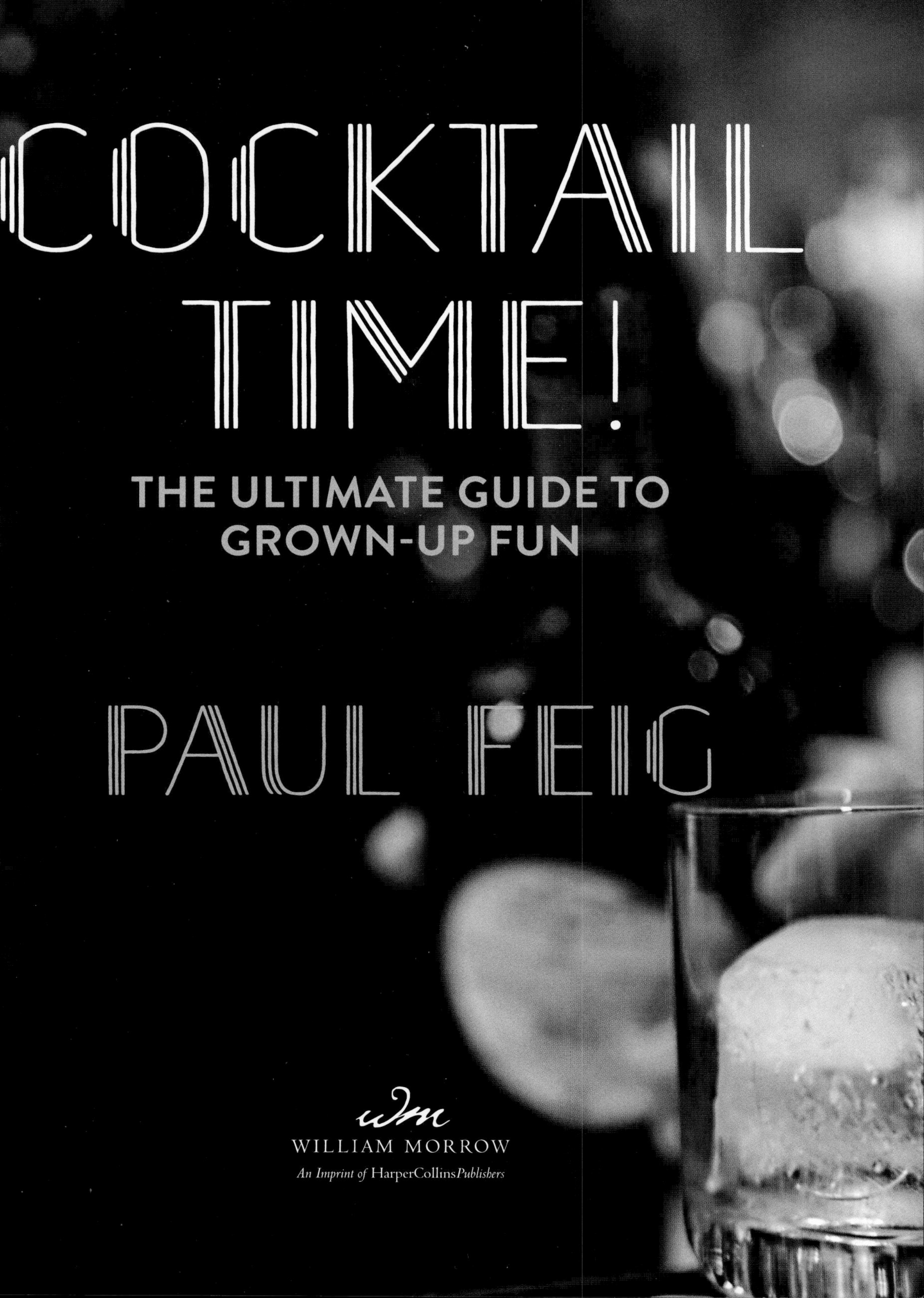

COCKTAIL TIME!

THE ULTIMATE GUIDE TO GROWN-UP FUN

PAUL FEIG

wm

WILLIAM MORROW

An Imprint of HarperCollins*Publishers*

TO LAURIE,
the Tipsy to my Funcle

AND

ALESSANDRO PALAZZI,
the maestro of the martini

CONTENTS

WELCOME TO THE PARTY!

ello, friend of grown-up fun and good taste! My name is Paul Feig, and I'm mostly known for writing, directing, and producing movies and television shows like *Bridesmaids*, *Spy*, and *Freaks and Geeks*, among many others. I was also a standup comedian and actor before that. You may remember me as Mr. Pool, the biology teacher from the first season of the ABC sitcom *Sabrina the Teenage Witch* back in the mid-1990s. Or as "guy eating turkey and dancing with headphones on" from a Louis Rich Turkey commercial I did in 1988. (It's on YouTube if you want to watch it.) Or . . . well, the list goes on.

But don't hold any of that against me. The thing I'd rather you know me for is my love of cocktails. I'm obsessed with them. But not just cocktails. I'm obsessed with cocktail culture and the cocktail lifestyle in general, because you can't have one without the other. Simply put, I love the aesthetics of all things booze—the glassware, the bottles, the bars, the bartenders and their mixology equipment. I love fancy high-end bars and I love great dive bars. There are few things more magical in the world to me than walking into a dimly lit watering hole where all the bottles are illuminated from below, creating a Kubrickian glow on the dark wood walls and shelves and throwing a romantic warmth over the cocktail-sipping patrons. To belly up to the bar and give my order to a friendly bartender and then pick up an ice-cold martini glass or feel the warmth of an old fashioned tumbler with a fresh pour of single-malt scotch in the bottom is like stepping through the gates of Valhalla and being asked, "What can we do to make your stay more comfortable?"

And so, for all these reasons and more, I wanted to write a book about cocktails. But to clarify, this is not a book filled with little-known facts about alcoholic drinks, their origins, and the history of mixology. That would require far too much work and research on my lazy butt's behalf, and it isn't where my interest lies. There are plenty of amazing books and websites dedicated to this subject; Ted Haigh, aka Dr. Cocktail, alone could and has filled volumes with his amazing facts and discoveries about all things mixed drinks. Nor is this a book about cutting-edge mixology and scientific bartending techniques. I won't be telling you, the reader, how to use a centrifuge to reduce a bottle of old wine into a paste or how to create vermouth smoke with an ionizer. There are several books about molecular mixology that are mind-bendingly inventive and imaginative, and some genius bartenders, like my good friend Todd Maul in Boston, can show you how to turn your home bar into a madman's laboratory of alcoholic delights that would make Einstein's head spin. But again, that's all way too much work to do when you just want to have a drink. Or at least it is for me.

No, none of that is what I'm doing here. I am not an expert. I am merely a guy who really, *really* loves cocktails and the lifestyle they represent, and one who wants to share that love with a world that has gotten away from what I consider to be the glory days of grown-up good times—cocktail parties; dressing up and having a fun night with friends as you sip libations; mixing yourself a perfect martini at home after a hard day at work. This book is as much about the fun that can be had from the cocktail lifestyle as it is a guide to making mixed drinks. Unlike my Instagram show, *Quarantine Cocktail Time!*, by which this book was inspired (we'll get to that in a minute), I wanted to write the layman's ultimate modern guide to making cocktails—and how you can most entertainingly use them to turn your social life into greatness. Writing this book has allowed me to go more in depth than I ever did on my show into (a) the things you'll need to make the drinks, (b) the things you can do to best present your drinks and yourself, and—most important—(c) how to make your cocktails the vehicle to becoming the classy, fun person you've always known you could be.

Look, you don't even have to drink alcohol to get true value out of this book. You can live the cocktail lifestyle by throwing a get-together and serving nonalcoholic beverages to an interesting and diverse group of well-dressed guests and still be the toast of your peers. You can go to any bar with people you know and order a spicy virgin Mary or a grapefruit and soda or any other nonalcoholic concoction and have as classy a good time as any alcohol drinkers. The fact that you're all sipping out of nice glasses while you mix and mingle in a fun grown-up setting is what matters. The cocktail lifestyle is all about being with friends and having great conversations. It's about putting on your best clothes and throwing smart and fun gatherings or heading to your favorite bar and having an interesting chat with the bartender. It can even be about staying home and mixing a drink in a beautiful glass to sip as you watch a great old movie by yourself. The fun is in the environment you create and what you make of it. The cocktail lifestyle merely means living life to its fullest, and I want to show you how to do it all with fun-loving aplomb. It's all here in *Cocktail Time!*—how to make the drinks, what glasses to serve them in, how to throw the parties, how to dress, what music to play. It's one-stop shopping for upgrading the fun in your life!

The genesis of this book came from the Covid-19 quarantine. When the lockdown began in March 2020, since I'm not a medical professional, I decided that my contribution to helping people during this terrible period in our nation's history would be to do an Instagram Live show every single day to raise money for first responders, essential workers, and coronavirus charities while trying to entertain my trapped-at-home viewers as I delved into cocktail books and made a different cocktail every day for one hundred days in a row.

During it all, I learned a lot about mixology by simply doing it every night. Before I came up with my show, my drink-making prowess was focused on martinis and Negronis. But I soon found myself becoming quite adept at whipping up all sorts of mixed drinks as I delved deeper and deeper into the cocktail world, and I had a blast in the process. I never made any drinks on the show that required a lot of advance preparation in the kitchen (and the subsequent mess that comes with it). I just wanted to make drinks that had fun ingredients my audience could find in their bar or pick up at a liquor store and throw together in a shaker or mixing glass,

that tasted great, and that got them to the party quicker. I learned so much about the different ingredients that can go into cocktails that I soon began inventing my own recipes, many of which are in the pages of *Cocktail Time!* (And I have also hit up some of my famous friends for their own favorite recipes to include in this book. People like Charlize Theron, Kerry Washington, Henry Golding, Kylie Minogue, Jenna Fischer, Angela Kinsey, Michelle Yeoh, Allison Janney, and more have joined me in these boozy pages.)

Cocktails and cocktail culture are the key to grown-up fun, and this book provides both the proof and the road map. Just think of all the amazing parties you and your friends are going to throw—soirees filled with fabulous cocktails and peopled by adults dressed in their finest and most fashionable, sipping and laughing and exchanging ideas and opinions. Escape your kids for the evening! Let the dog have a night without you in his space on the couch! Break out your suits and cocktail dresses! It's time to party!!! Good lord, it's almost too much to think about! Cheers, and away we go!!!

Paul Feig,
your own personal Drunk Funcle

BEFORE YOU START BOOZIN'...

Look, how you drink is up to you. If you want to drink wine out of a plastic cup, be my guest. I'm your Drunk Funcle, emphasis on the *fun* part, and so I'm not going to lecture you or judge you the way so many people have lectured and judged me in my life, like the time my dad yelled at me and forced me to put on my galoshes in front of everybody at the bus stop because I snuck out of the house without them. But I can tell you that drinking isn't just about the alcohol going down your throat and the buzz it can give you. That's part of it, and it's part of the fun, too, if you do it responsibly. Drinking, however, should be about the full experience. It should be as much about the aesthetics and the feel and the savoring of this wonderful gift the gods gave us so many eons ago when they created the process of distillation and fermentation as it is about tossing back booze.

If you watch any of my movies, you'll find that several of them have a scene in a bar, and you'll notice that I always uplight the bottles, meaning we have them on glass shelves with light strips underneath or behind them so that the bottles glow like the beautiful vessels they are. Whether the bar is a dive (*The Heat*) or in an elegant casino (*Spy*), the bottles are the focus. In *A Simple Favor*, Blake Lively makes a perfect Dukes Bar martini, and the comment I've heard the most about that movie is how everyone is dying for a martini the second that scene comes on the screen.

Sure, cocktails are about the booze and the high they can give you. But they're as much about the bottles and the glasses and the surroundings and the people and, most important, *you* and how you face all of it. It's your chance to have fun—adult fun—and you should make it as special as possible. So follow me, and I'll give you a few pointers on how to make it the best experience it can be, no matter where you're enjoying your drink.

EVERY DRINK SHOULD BE SPECIAL

J ust because you're drinking at home doesn't mean it can't feel like you're in the world's coolest bar. Look at some pictures from the 1950s and '60s of cocktail parties people held in their apartments. Everyone is decked out in formal wear, looking suave and elegant in tuxedoes and gowns, while sitting crammed onto a couch in someone's small dwelling sipping cocktails. And it just looks glamorous as hell.

Whether you're throwing a party at your house or just having a drink with your significant other (or even having one by yourself!), treat each and every libation as the special occasion it is. Bring the ritual, the artistry, and the beauty to each glass

of booze you enjoy. Make it feel as special as it would if you were dropping a bunch of money to sit in a fancy bar served by a seasoned professional bartender. Make that drink a celebration of life and accomplishment, a beautiful reward for a day well used.

I know for me the idea of a martini or other mixed drink is the thing that gets me through even the toughest of days. On my movies, I shoot what is known in the business as French hours. What that means is we shoot for ten hours straight through, with no lunch other than food that's passed around the set all day so that people won't get hungry, and then at the end of the ten hours we pull the plug and everyone goes home to their families and has a nice evening of dinner and, if they want, drinks. From a production standpoint, it means that you don't have a cast and crew who are bleary-eyed and falling asleep on their feet and who subsequently don't fall asleep on the drive home (a very real and tragic thing that happens more than you would think when you have crews working sixteen- to eighteen-hour days all week). It also means we get more done in a shorter amount of time, because when you shut down for a one-hour lunch, it's usually more like an hour and a half, and then it takes another hour for everyone to get back up to speed. So for me, French hours are the most civilized way to work and the surest way to get a gin-filled glass in my hand in the shortest amount of time.

But enough showbiz talk! My point is that cocktail time should be a special time. The drinks you make, how you make them, how you serve them, and how you enjoy them are all part of the fun.

How do you do it all? Well, it's quite simple if you have the right tools and the right attitude . . .

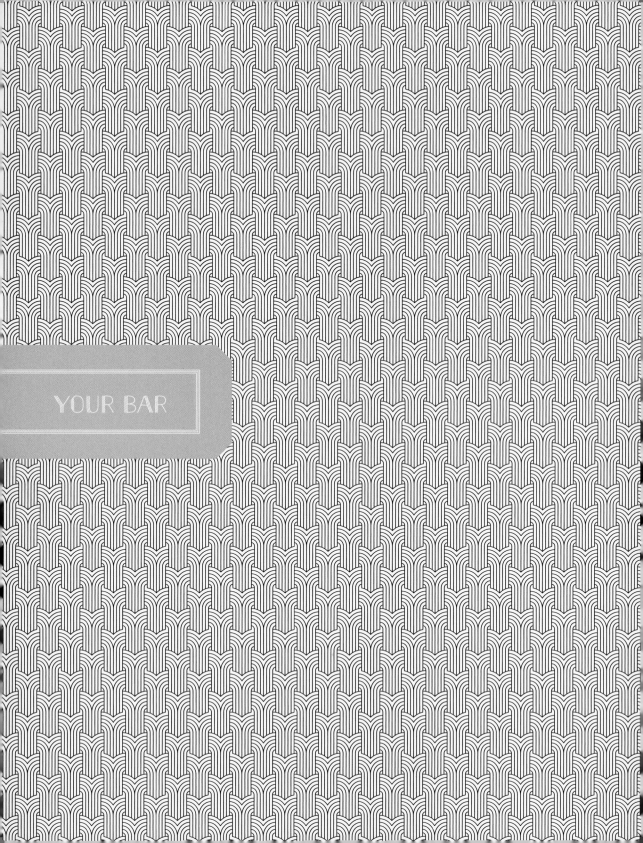

YOUR BAR

The term *bar* is one that conjures up many different images in many different people's minds. As a kid growing up in Detroit, Michigan, I knew only that bars were places that my parents and I would drive past and that often had no windows but always seemed to have intriguing names. They were either puns or jokes like "The Pour House" and "On the Rocks" or intimidating guys' names like "Joe's" or "Sam's" or "Rocko's."

In a twist of supreme irony, I was raised a Christian Scientist by two religious parents who never touched a drop of alcohol. And so bars were forbidden and looked-down-upon places when I was growing up. All the cop shows of the 1970s that my friends and I would watch—*Baretta, Cannon, Starsky and Hutch,* and so on—always had scenes in tough dive bars where the heroes would find some criminal or stool pigeon and a fight would usually ensue. So my fear of bars only grew. It wasn't until I hit drinking age and started confronting my misconceptions that I would finally figure out that all bars are not created equal.

The biggest eye-opening moment for me was when I first went to London with my future wife, Laurie, when I was in my late twenties. We'd both been living in Los Angeles for several years, and the bar scene was still all about windowless establishments where drinking was hidden from the outside world. Cocktails were enjoyed in a darkened room, without the eyes of the people on the other side of the walls watching you. Imagine my confusion when I found myself walking down a street in Central London and saw a huge crowd of people holding glasses and standing out on the sidewalk around 5:30 p.m. Unsure if there had been some kind of fire drill or evacuation, I walked over to investigate. What I found was the after-work crowd at their favorite pub, having a pint or a G&T or a glass of wine with their friends, chatting and laughing about the day's work and life in general.

Looking more closely at the pub, I saw that it wasn't a windowless watering hole. This pub had huge windows that had been slid open for fresh air and outside tables and a shelf built onto the front of the outer facade that people could rest their drinks on. Inside, it was lots of wood and lights and fun old signs and carpeting and booths and tables and it was just so full of life and laughter that I wasn't sure if I had wandered into a private party at someone's house.

But no. This was just how people drank in London. It wasn't a place of shame like the bars back in the United States or the ones I had observed on TV as a kid—dark holes-in-the-wall where people hunched over drinks and boozed their troubles away, eventually ending up threatening one another with broken bottles and breaking pool cues over one another's heads.

This was just a nightly celebration of life and getting by. There were even a few kids in there with their parents, the kids sipping sodas while their folks enjoyed their libations. There was no Puritanical shame, no hiding the drinkers from the outside world, no losing track of what time it was because you can't see if there's still daylight outside or not. It made me realize what a judgmental view of drinking my home country of America had. And it opened my eyes to just what booze can be about if it's consumed responsibly, in moderation, and with a mature point of view.

So why give you a lecture about attitudes toward drinking when I was supposed to be telling you how to set up your home bar? Well, I guess I just want you to face it with what I consider to be the healthy attitude toward cocktails. Making, sharing, and consuming cocktails should be fun. That's it. That's all. There's no shame in it.

Cocktail time is fun time, a time to unwind and socialize and laugh and take a break from your busy life.

This should all be reflected in your bar. It can be a big built-in area in your house, with stools and a countertop and shelves behind it for bottles and glasses; it can be a cool bar cart that you have against the wall or tucked into a corner; it can be a tray with glasses, bar tools, and your favorite spirits on a table or ottoman; or it can just be a cupboard in your kitchen where you have what you need to make your favorite tipple. Whatever it is and whatever size it is, it needs to make you happy.

THE GLASSES

For me, the first step is the glasses. The glass you drink a cocktail out of is basically the clothing for your tipple. Sure, some people dress simply to cover themselves so they don't get arrested for indecent exposure. This is the equivalent of drinking a cocktail out of a red plastic Solo cup. You can do it, and you may enjoy the drink and get the same buzz from it, but it's not a very impressive way of going about things. That kind of drinking

is just function over form. I think form is as important as—sometimes even more important than—function, and while I've never been a strict form-over-function guy, I've always thought the best way to run your life is to have form and function work in harmony with each other.

Now, some of you might think this all sounds very pretentious and elitist. Maybe it is. But there's also nothing wrong with wanting things to be nice sometimes. One of the things I did in my twenties that still makes me cringe to remember is from when I was in a rebellious phase with my relationship to Hollywood and to Los Angeles in general. A couple of friends invited me to eat with them at a fancy Santa Monica hot spot. Feeling like a rebel, I decided that I would show those pretentious elites who dined there a thing or two by strutting in wearing shorts, an old Hawaiian shirt, and dirty sneakers. I remember parading in with a superior air through the nicely dressed crowd and sitting down at our table. My friends were immediately put off and asked me what I thought I was doing. I proudly said that I didn't want to be pretentious like all these other people. I was sure I had the moral high ground. But I very quickly realized I was just being a flaming asshole as I looked around at the parties of nicely dressed people, families out for a fun evening or birthday celebration, couples out on a date night, and others who were just trying to have an overall pleasant, semi-elegant time. I was some low-rent rebel making a meritless point, and my greatest accomplishment was ruining everyone else's evening by looking like shit.

If you want to drink like you're at a kegger at a frat house, go right ahead. All I can say is that when you mix a martini and pour it into a nice frosty martini glass, you get a thrill. I know that I do. Even if you're at home by yourself in your pajamas or sweatpants, picking up a cold Nick and Nora glass filled with a perfectly mixed and chilled cocktail makes you feel like you're in the world's classiest nightclub. You

feel cooler. You feel like an adult. And you simply enjoy the drink more.

Look, again, I'm not here to judge. But I have to assume that if you're reading this book and are familiar with the lifestyle I enjoy, you don't mind stepping up your game. So step up your glass game first. It doesn't mean you have to head to Baccarat and drop a month's salary on a set of cut-crystal glasses. You can find nice cocktail glasses in a lot of different places—department stores, big-box retailers, thrift shops, secondhand stores, or online—nice cocktail glasses (or glasses you can use for cocktails) are everywhere.

I've bought a lot of glasses over the years at restaurant-supply stores. You usually have to buy them in sets of six or twelve, but professional barware is made to be very durable, so it's perfect for parties. It's designed to take some abuse from all the washing, manhandling, and excess use it all goes through each night. So the glasses look good but aren't so fragile that you end up breaking one or two of them when you're washing up after a long evening. I've had some elegant, expensive wineglasses over the years with gorgeous thin stems and paper-thin bowls that literally snap into pieces the minute you put a sponge inside to try to wash them. Now all my guests get restaurant wineglasses that you could pretty much drop from the top of a ladder onto cement and they'd simply bounce once and be ready for a refill.

As I mentioned, you can also find some real gems in thrift shops and secondhand stores—classic old cocktail glasses that get buried on the shelves with all the other old water glasses and dishes. It's also fun to find glasses that you can use as unexpected substitutes for the standard cocktail-glass shapes. Almost any tall glass can function as a highball glass, so find ones with shapes and patterns that make you smile.

It's also very fun to go on eBay and type in "vintage cocktail glasses." While you may end up paying a bit more than you would at a thrift store, you'll have a better chance of finding some truly unique old glasses from the days when companies were making much more elaborate drinking vessels. The 1950s and '60s were a particularly cool time, with companies like Culver making glasses with cool shiny-paint geometric designs that sometimes even came with their own carrying rack so it was easier to pass them around at parties (an idea that definitely needs a revival).

As you can see, you have many options for making sure your drinks are housed in the most appealing containers.

My only plea to you is this—please don't drink alcohol out of plastic. I get the necessity if you're at a pool party and it's too risky to have glassware that could break and cut somebody's foot open. But beyond that, it's just not serving anyone well. Plastic can't get cold enough and stay cold enough to keep your drink nice and frosty. Wine from a plastic cup just feels wrong when you sip it, and frankly, those cups always smell a bit weird. There's something about the weight of a glass actually *made* of glass in your hand and on your lips when you drink from it that just feels right. Trust me on this one. Booze sipped from plastic is never fantastic. You can quote me on that.

The foundational glasses that will give you the most flexibility without overstuffing your bar are:

2 TO 4 MARTINI GLASSES, NICK AND NORA GLASSES, OR COCKTAIL COUPES

I'll talk more (and more passionately) about glass size when I discuss martinis, but for now, it's best to get smaller glasses that hold around 4 to 5 ounces versus the 8- to 10-ounce martini glasses that are found everywhere these days. Smaller glasses are more civilized and also help keep your drinks cold because they're not so huge that it takes longer to drink them.

I'd also advise against stemless martini glasses, either the kind with short stumpy bases or the ones that have no stem and sit inside a round base that holds

ice. Also, avoid glasses with kooky bent or zigzag stems. You want to be able to hold a martini glass by the stem, if you desire, in order to keep your hand from warming up the drink.

In other words—go traditional. Let the drink be the topic of conversation, not the glass. It's like the late McLean Stevenson said to me once when I was an actor on a show with him and the costume people wanted my character to wear a wacky outfit—"You can either walk through a door funny, or you can walk through a funny door. Better to walk through a door funny, because anyone can do it the other way." Your drinks are no different.

2 TO 4 HIGHBALL OR TOM COLLINS GLASSES

These are your most versatile glasses, by far. So much so that it might be worth getting 6 or 8 of them. You can serve pretty much any drink in these, whether it has ice or not. If you watch old movies from the 1930s and '40s, you'll see people pouring all kinds of booze into these glasses, everything from scotch and soda to straight whiskey and brandy. The highball glass is a bit wider than a Tom Collins glass and so is the most sensible of the two, if you must pick one, because it can also double as a water glass at the dinner table. Tom Collins glasses tend to be narrower and a bit taller. But both are great and can handle anything that isn't supposed to be in a martini glass. They're also good for your friends who don't drink alcohol, because they can enjoy a club soda, juice, or soft drink out of these and still look like part of the party.

2 TO 4 OLD FASHIONED GLASSES

Next to martini glasses, these are my favorite shape of glasses. They just look and feel very cool and grown-up in your hand. Truth be told, I really enjoy a glass of single-malt scotch, and whenever I have one, I always have it in an old fashioned glass. I love the way it feels in my hand, the way it balances when I swirl the liquid in the bottom of the glass. It's one of the most mature glasses a person can hold. I also make a lot of mixed drinks in old fashioned glasses. It's my go-to glass for Negronis and whiskey sours on the rocks. Pretty much any drink that is served over ice can be enjoyed in an old fashioned glass. I personally like ones with heavy bases because they feel more substantial in your hand. If the glass is too light it downplays the nice whiskey or cocktail inside it. But it's all personal taste, so the best thing to do is go to a store and try picking a few up from the shelf to see which one feels right for you before you buy it.

2 TO 4 MEDIUM-SIZE WINEGLASSES

The world of wineglasses is as varied as the cocktail glass world times ten. If you really love wine, you'll end up getting glasses that best accent the myriad different varietals of red and white, like Bordeaux and Pinot Noirs, Rieslings and Chardonnays, and so on and so on. To be honest, the list of different glasses you can amass as a wine connoisseur is a little ridiculous. It's also part of the fun. But for starting out purposes, if you've got limited space and resources, a medium-size white wine glass works fine for reds, whites, and sparkling varieties. (As a matter of fact, a lot of sommeliers now prefer serving Champagne in white wine glasses as opposed to Champagne flutes, so serving bubbles to your guests in a wineglass will make them think you're extra classy and in the know!)

Of course, you're always going to encounter some wine aficionado who hates putting a pricier red into what they consider to be a white wine glass, and I totally get that. But this size of glass will get the job done and keep you from having a thousand different glasses and, trust me, the wine will taste just as good in it, assuming it's actually good wine. It's more about the wine itself and how and when you open it and pour it than it is about the glass.

There are volumes of books about wine and the infinite rules about how to serve it, and this book is called *Cocktail Time!*, so I'll defer to those other sources.

But I'll share one tip that will help you pass the sniff test with any wine lover, something I learned during an embarrassing incident in an Indian restaurant in London many years ago. I was out to dinner with several friends who had flown in from the United States, and one of them brought along the brother of a French friend of ours. He was a bit of an oddball and a hothead and the rest of us were sitting there hoping he wouldn't cause some kind of scene. We were getting on with the evening until the poor waiter came over with a bottle of wine this man had ordered. The waiter waited for him to taste it and, once he approved of it, poured him a glass. Our acquaintance went ballistic and started dressing down the waiter. I didn't know what the problem was until our friend's brother picked up the wineglass and pointed at its side. "Never pour wine past the widest part of the glass!" he yelled. "You'll crush the wine!" That's when I saw that the waiter had poured the glass about two-thirds full—definitely past the widest part of the glass. We were all embarrassed at the outburst, but I can now say that our rude dinner companion was sort of right.

While I find the idea of "crushing the wine" to be rather dubious, I agree that it's always best not to fill a wineglass past that curve. It makes the glass look too full, and it also means you're going through your bottle too quickly. I have a personal pet peeve in restaurants when the waiter keeps coming to the table and topping off our wineglasses when we still have enough in them, because I know they're just trying to drain the bottle to get us to order another one. Sometimes they'll overfill the glass to kill off the final inch in the bottom of the bottle. It's not cool to do this, and you're well within your rights as a customer to call them on it if they do. Wine is to be savored and enjoyed at your own pace; there's no call for you to be chugging it just so the restaurateurs can up their profits for the night.

Side note: One of my favorite gags in relation to this was when I directed the "Dinner Party" episode of *The Office*. The character of Dwight brought a bottle of red and two big wineglasses to the party, so I had him fill his glass almost all the way to the top with wine, which a maximalist like Dwight would probably do. It was a joke

only a wine lover would get, but it still makes me laugh heartily when I remember Rainn Wilson picking up this enormous glass of wine and taking a sip off the top. I think it was my long-awaited revenge against that French guy for embarrassing us in the restaurant. Booze humor!

All that said, if you are also able get a few larger red wine glasses, you can use them to serve Aperol spritzes, gin and tonics, gin and sodas, and similar drinks, which until recent years were always served in highball glasses. I'm all for it. You can get more ice as well as more booze into these bigger glasses, and since they're hot-weather drinks, it's nice not to have to go back for constant refills. You can keep the drink colder longer by picking it up by the stem instead of holding the sides of the glass, which makes the ice melt faster. Also, spritzes are inherently pretty drinks because of their color, and a wineglass makes the perfect showcase, like a painting with a nice frame.

So to wrap up . . .

Sure, there's a ton of other shapes and sizes of glasses with which you can stock a bar. I guarantee that once you get your bar all set up and filled in, you'll slowly begin to amass other types of glasses. But to start, your martini/cocktail glasses will accommodate all your drinks that are served straight up (like martinis, Manhattans, and Cosmos), your highball/Tom Collins glasses will accommodate all your mixed drinks that have ice in them (like Tom Collins, gin and tonics, and tequila sunrises), the old fashioned glasses will work with shorter iced drinks (like Negronis, whiskey sours, and scotch and sodas), and the wineglasses can work with wine, Champagne, and spritzes.

If you have these four shapes in your bar, you'll be ready for anything.

THE GEAR

Just like with glasses, it's really easy to amass a ton of gadgets and doohickeys for every possible purpose under the sun. I've got everything from an electric swizzle stick to some evil-looking trident thing that you use to unstick a swollen Champagne cork. But the reality is you don't need a ton of stuff. A lot of gadgets are single-purpose items that perform a function that could easily be done with an existing kitchen tool. Peelers that make little curlicue lemon twists, muddlers that crush fruit in your shaker, canvas Lewis bags with wooden mallets you use to make cracked ice—you could improvise versions of these just fine if you took a tour through your kitchen's drawers and cupboards.

Here's the simplest list possible of things to start with, so you don't have to spend a fortune getting your home bar up and running . . .

THE ABSOLUTE ESSENTIALS

Items you simply can't make cocktails without

COCKTAIL SHAKER—The shape known as a cobbler, which is in three pieces—the main shaker, the top with a strainer in it, and a cap for the strainer—is the most versatile, so it would be a good choice for your first shaker. There are other styles of shakers that I love, like the Parisian shaker, but this workhorse will never let you down if you get a decent one. (More on this when you turn the page.)

JIGGER—Get one with measurement lines that measure up to two ounces and in increments of ½, 1, and 1½ ounces. Make it as easy on yourself as possible when mixing drinks so you don't have to guess at how much you're pouring. The measurements in most recipes are very precise, so anything you can do to take the guesswork out of measuring will only make your cocktails better.

LONG-HANDLED COCKTAIL STIRRING SPOON—The kind with a thin, twisted metal shaft is best. They're the easiest to stir with, especially when you need to spin the spoon to keep the back of its bowl against the inside wall of the shaker. Some spoons have a fork on the end, others a muddler, but I prefer a simple teardrop at the top. You can use this end for stirring drinks like Negronis when the spoon end may have trouble getting past the ice in the glass.

WINE OPENER/BOTTLE OPENER—My favorite is what's known as the waiter's wine opener. It has a bottle opener, a small blade for cutting the foil off the top of a wine bottle, a corkscrew, and a jointed arm that allows you to pull the cork out in two swift moves by pulling half the cork out first, then readjusting the joint onto the lip of the bottle to pull the cork out the rest of the way.

ICE TRAYS—You can't really have cocktails without ice, but you already knew that. I would suggest getting trays that say the ice comes out of them easily. A small tip: Don't overfill your trays. Ice comes out easier if they're not overflowing. Take it from someone who usually overfills the trays and ends up with cracked and chipped ice. (If your refrigerator has an icemaker, you can always use that ice for inside your cocktail shaker, but I'm not a fan of the half-moon shaped cubes they usually produce. Square or rectangle cubes look much nicer in a glass and also look like you put a bit more effort into your mixology. Also, since they are bigger, they melt more slowly and won't dilute your drink as quickly. My advice? Make your own.)

Sure, that headline below sounds like a war of second-tier superheroes, but it's really about the three different kinds of shakers and which one is best for you. I suggest the cobbler as the most versatile shaker because it's the one that's most complete, having its strainer built into the top. When a cobbler works, it's great. But there are a lot of shitty cobbler shakers on the market, and it's hard to tell until you get one of them home whether it's a good one or not. The biggest problem is that a lot of them leak when you shake them, either through the join between the bottom half and the lid or through the join between the lid and the strainer cap. And it's not a price thing. One of my most expensive art deco cobblers from a very top brand leaks like a sieve when I shake it. If you're buying online, look at the reviews and see what people say. As we all know, nobody holds back in those online product reviews.

A Boston shaker is basically two mixing tins that you fit together. They're the ones you see all bartenders using and they work great, but they're also a bit tricky to master because you have to make sure they're sealed together tightly before you shake, and they're also sometimes really hard to pull apart after you shake.

My personal favorite? A Parisian shaker. It's the best of both worlds. It gives you the tight seal of a Boston shaker but with the ease of a cobbler when you pull it apart after shaking. The only reason I didn't flag it as the one to get is that you'll need to buy a strainer to pour out your drink because there isn't one built into the top like in a cobbler. So, if you're up for spending the extra money to get a strainer, then it's the Parisian shaker all the way! Ooo la la!!!

THE COBBLER VERSUS THE BOSTON VERSUS THE PARISIAN

THE SECONDARY ESSENTIALS

*Items you could find in your kitchen but are great to have
dedicated at your bar*

- **COCKTAIL STRAINER**—fits over the mouth of your shaker
  for easy pouring
- **SHARP PARING KNIFE**—for cutting lemons and limes
- **SMALL CUTTING BOARD**—so you don't
  get your bar top all sticky
- **HANDHELD CITRUS JUICER/PRESS**—
  for squeezing lemons and limes

THE NEXT WAVE

*The little extras that will make your cocktail
mixing much more convenient*

- **ICE BUCKET**—so you don't have to keep running to the
  freezer for more cubes
- **ICE SCOOP OR LARGE METAL SPOON**—because you
  never want to use your hands to put ice into a
  shaker or glass when making drinks for other
  people

- **MIXING GLASS**—a more elegant and
  entertaining way to mix stirred drinks
- **A FEW BAR TOWELS**—because no matter how
  hard you try not to, you're going to make a mess

- **MUDDLER**—to crush fruit and herbs in the bottom of
  your shaker for certain recipes. It's better to use a wooden
  muddler, because the metal ones will break a glass shaker or
  mixing glass if you try to muddle in it. Trust me, I speak
  from experience.

That's about it. The Absolute Essentials are all very flexible and multipurpose if you really consider them. A cocktail shaker does a lot of things. You can mix all the ingredients in it, either by shaking or stirring, you can crush fruit or herbs in the bottom of it, and you can use the strainer in the top to filter out everything from the shaker into the cocktail glass. The jigger obviously allows you to measure the exact amounts of whatever your drink recipes call for. A mixing spoon is for drinks you don't shake. The bottle opener . . . well, it opens bottles. And the ice trays? I don't think I need to explain unless you like your cocktails room temperature.

To be honest, if you only had a shaker and a jigger, you could still make cocktails as long as you have access to the other standard tools in your kitchen. Even though I listed a long-handled cocktail mixing spoon, you can use anything to stir a drink, from a regular spoon to a knife to a chopstick (which I've done on many occasions when I've made drinks at someone else's spoonless house). You need a wine opener to open wine, but if you're just going to make cocktails, most booze bottles have screw tops or corked caps you can pull out by hand, unless you've found some odd spirit or liqueur that has a wine-corked top (but those are few and far between). And you can always just buy ice at the convenience store instead of making your own.

However, to limit your running around gathering things when you want to make a drink, it's always nice to have those tools permanently on your bar. It's just up to you how much money you want to spend up front.

The same goes for the Secondary Essentials. You can just use the strainer in the lid of your cobbler shaker to pour drinks, but it's usually much easier to do it with a separate strainer, especially for stirred drinks, and you definitely need one if you're using a mixing glass or a Parisian shaker. You must have some knives in your kitchen, so you can just use one of those to cut your lemons and limes and twists, but it's nice to have one dedicated at your bar so you don't have to go searching through drawers or the dishwasher to find one. You can always squeeze your lemons and limes by hand into the jigger if you don't want to spend money on a juicer. And you can always just cut fruit on the counter or your kitchen cutting board, but it's nice to have a small board sitting there on your bar ready and waiting to go.

As for the Next Wave items, you can muddle fruit and herbs using the handle end of a wooden spoon, and you can put your ice in a regular bowl and scoop it out with a serving spoon, and you can use the bottom half of your shaker for stirring drinks instead of doing it in a mixing glass, and you can use paper towels to clean up. But, again, it's sort of nice to have those dedicated items at your bar if you're up for spending a few extra bucks. It'll just make you feel more like an aficionado and look more professional to your guests. And what's wrong with that?

THE BOOZE

Okay, now we enter a territory known as a slippery slope.

Depending on the kind of cocktails you enjoy, you could get away with just a few bottles of different liquors. If you only like martinis, you can get away with just two bottles of booze—gin or vodka and vermouth. If you like to dip into other classic cocktails, like Manhattans and Negronis, you're going to need a few more bottles. And if you decide you want to start playing with different recipes from cocktail books, well, your collection of bottles is going to grow exponentially.

When I started *Quarantine Cocktail Time!* on my Instagram Live feed during the lockdown, I had a nice selection of standard bottles of booze. The shelves of my bar were comfortably inhabited by a solid number of gins, vodkas, scotches, tequilas, and Cognacs, along with a few more popular mixers like Campari, Aperol, and Cointreau. But then as I started plowing through my old copy of *Mr. Boston* and all the other cocktail recipe books I own and saw all the ingredients I was missing, I started ordering more and more bottles from Drizly, who would dutifully deliver them to my house. As I approached our one hundredth episode, Laurie said that our bar area looked like a booze hoarder's house. And she wasn't exaggerating. I now have one of the best-stocked cocktail test kitchens in all the land. But it's also a little ridiculous.

There are just so many types of liquors, liqueurs, fortified wines, bitters, and other fun things you can put into cocktails that your bar can quickly start to look like a liquor store if you decide to really go for it. I now have bottles of kümmel, apry, Swedish punsch, crème de violette, crème de cacao, crème de noyaux, and tons of other kinds of crèmes and flavored liqueurs rightfully placed beside my original main staples. And even those staples have an endless number of brands and varietals. The opportunity for you to turn your house into a bottle museum is very, very high if you really start to enjoy mixology.

So what should you do? If you're starting out, I say it's best to go for the basics. Think about the cocktails you like and that you're most interested in perfecting and stick to those for now. I've spent years perfecting my martinis, and as I mentioned, those have only two boozy ingredients. It's always best to start out with the simple goal of being a master of one or two drinks before you try to head into the Jack-of-All-Trades department. One perfect drink is more impressive to people than a bunch of simply good drinks.

However, if your goal is to entertain and make cocktails for your guests, and you'd like to be able to field their more diverse requests, then get a bottle of gin, a bottle of vodka, a bottle of rum, a bottle of tequila, and a bottle of whiskey. Add two bottles of vermouth, one sweet and dark and one dry and light. Get a bottle of Angostura bitters and, if you're at all drawn to Negronis, a bottle of Campari or some other brand of Italian bitter liqueur. Add a bottle of simple syrup (or make your own—see page 112) and some lemons and limes, and you'll be able to make your guests enough different cocktails to impress even the most seasoned drinker.

Here's the thing—to have a truly complete cocktail bar, you'd need an endless supply of ingredients. You need to drill down a bit and decide what you want to serve and what will be most in demand when people come to your house, so that you can be poised for success. With the above group of bottles, you can make anybody a straight-up rocks drink (vodka rocks, whiskey rocks), a martini (gin or vodka), a Manhattan, or a Negroni. With the addition of the simple syrup and citrus, you can make whiskey sours, Tom Collinses, gimlets, daiquiris, and a lot of other fun

drinks that people like. Then, if you add in mixers like soda water, tonic water, and cola, you can make gin and tonics (or my favorite low-cal drink, a gin and soda), rum and Cokes, whiskey sodas, and more.

Your bar should be what you want it to be. Your goal is to please your guests and help them have a good time, and it's tempting to want to be the person who has people over and says, "What do you want to drink? I can make you anything." But you're just opening yourself up to frustration and humiliation if someone responds, "Can you make me an Only-Available-in-the-Most-Finicky-Hipster-Bar-in-the-World cocktail?" And you won't have the super-obscure ingredients it calls for and you'll have to admit defeat and they'll look at you disappointedly and everyone will be uncomfortable and unsatisfied.

It was like the time in junior high when I brought in my electric guitar to play with some other kids in front of our class. I thought I was going to crush it and impress the hell out of everybody with my skills. I got up and played along with the band, doing what I thought was quite an impressive guitar solo. The class watched me impassively, and I suddenly worried that maybe I had overestimated my talent. Then a kid none of us had ever really noticed asked if he could take a turn using my guitar. I said sure, figuring he would do some rudimentary strumming, but then the kid cranked up my amp and did a wailing guitar solo as if he had just been possessed by the spirit of Eddie Van Halen. My classmates went wild and everyone fell in love with him and he got a standing ovation and I had to do the Walk of Shame back up onstage to retrieve my stupid guitar and slink back to my desk like the underachiever I actually was.

So set up your bar, and hence yourself, for success. Figure out the drinks you and your friends enjoy and stock your bar with that menu in mind. There's nothing wrong with saying, "What can I get you? I can make you a martini, a Negroni, a whiskey sour, a daiquiri, a G&T, a Tom Collins, a rum and Coke, or anything on the rocks with water or soda that you'd like." I guarantee that list right there will blow their minds. People are used to going to other people's houses and being offered cheap wine in plastic cups and bottles of beer and maybe stumbling across some huge sad bottle of vodka from Costco standing on the kitchen counter like a lonely thirteen-year-old who's taller than everybody else standing by themself in the corner at the school dance. It's the fact that you have the ingredients, you know how to make the drink, you can present the drink beautifully, and you have taken the time to provide this grown-up fun for your friends that will make the biggest impression. Let your bar show your friends who you really are—a mature, responsible adult who knows how to have a good time and who makes sure that everybody else does, too.

Then, as you discover new drinks that sound like something you and your guests might like, you can slowly expand your bottle count. But at the end of the day, cocktails shouldn't be about showmanship. They should be about having a good time and letting your guests see that you want them to have as much fun as possible.

THE OTHER STUFF

The final pieces of the puzzle, which we discussed a bit above, are the mixers and the garnishes. Lemons, limes, oranges, olives, club soda, tonic water, carbonated drinks, simple syrup, sliced fruit, cocktail cherries, mint leaves, edible flowers, herbs, bamboo umbrellas, swizzle sticks, plastic monkeys . . . the list goes on and on.

Mixers give you more versatility in your drink making. I've found that people don't really require a wealth of booze options, but they do get very finicky about micro-variations of mixers. Whiskey goes with club soda or water, and gin and vodka can go with tonic or soda. Rum and whiskey can go with Coke, and whiskey can go with 7-Up, and on and on. So if you're throwing a party, it's best to stock up on mixers. Tossing in things like grenadine and Torani syrups and fruit juices like orange, grapefruit, and cranberry can expand things even further and help to make sure that everyone can have some kind of mixed drink that makes them happy. (And it gives the nondrinkers at your party more variety for their nonalcoholic evening.)

Cocktail aficionados want their drinks to be authentic, and non-aficionados just want to enjoy their favorite booze with a mixer they like. Both types of people are right, because whatever they like is what's right for them. Don't be a judgmental host. The person who wants a Jack & Cherry Coke is just as deserving of your respect as the person who wants a perfect dry martini.

As the host and drink maker, you are there to please, not judge. The only thing you should be judging is whether or not everybody feels comfortable, satisfied, and is having a great time. Judge yourself, not your guests.

As for garnishes, well, a great drink in a nice glass is really nice enough. But garnishes can put it over the top. Depending on the flavor of the drink, a twist, lime wheel, or orange slice can spruce things up. If you've got fun cocktail picks, spearing a maraschino cherry or some fruit and laying it across the top of the glass or dropping it in will add another dimension. Putting edible flowers or long fruit spears into a fruity drink can only add to the visual appeal. And a plastic monkey hung over the side of a glass will never fail to delight your guests.

Again, cocktails are all about having fun. They can be the catalyst to allowing people to be their most fun selves. So do as much or as little as you want when you're making drinks. Let your personality shine through, even if it's a side of your personality you are normally too shy to show. If you're rather introverted but hand somebody a delicious cocktail that's adorned with interesting garnishes and they find out you made it yourself, they'll immediately look at you in a different light, and you'll have something to talk about. You'll be the kid who did the wailing guitar solo. You're fun, and you want them to have fun. And that will get any party started.

Cocktail cherries, or maraschino cherries, are preserved marasca cherries that are stored in a sweet syrup sometimes spiked with brandy or other kinds of spirits. Some of the best brands are Luxardo, Fabbri Amarena, and Griottines. They have an intense cherry flavor, and the syrup can be drizzled into your drink to give it an extra cherry punch. They're also lovely to eat once you've finished your drink, like a little dessert at the end of your boozy meal.

True maraschino cherries are not to be confused with those nuclear red things that you find in Shirley Temples or on top of banana splits with those long stems that some people know how to tie a knot in with their tongues. People call them maraschinos, but these unfortunate cherries have been bleached in sulfur dioxide, hardened in calcium carbonate, dyed red with coal tar, and flavored with benzaldehyde. Yum!

THE BIRDS AND THE BEES ABOUT COCKTAIL CHERRIES

Unless you need one of those nasty things to impress someone with your tongue skills or you like the look of it in your drink, steer clear of them. They're filled with awful stuff, they don't really taste like cherries, and I read somewhere that they stay in your colon for a couple of years. I've never been able to confirm that last part, but to be on the safe side, just use real maraschino cherries in your drinks. Your body will thank you.

HOW TO MAKE SURE EVERYBODY HAS FUN . . . INCLUDING YOU!

How big should your cocktail party be? Who should you invite to your cocktail party? What is the purpose of your cocktail party? How much do you have to do beyond providing the cocktails? How can you make sure people have the most fun possible? These are all questions worth thinking about before you pull the booze trigger.

We all have different definitions about what makes for a good party. Some of us like big parties. Others prefer intimate get-togethers. Some of us love to meet new people. Others are too shy to enjoy themselves around strangers. Some of our friends don't mix particularly well with other friends of ours.

I walk the line on all the above. I tend to dread big parties, but once I'm there I'm usually happy I went. I've definitely had some of my most embarrassing moments at big parties, though. Once at a Golden Globes party, I got so nervous being around so many stars that I downed several martinis in quick succession to try to calm down and ended up introducing myself to Meryl

Streep not once, not twice, but *three* times, each time forgetting that I had done it the previous time. (Laurie was only too happy to alert me to this fact after the third introduction.) Another time I was at an Oscar party and my hero Mick Jagger was there. Vowing not to drink that night so I wouldn't tri-introduce myself to any stars, I told my agent at the time that I was too nervous to say hi to Mick. My agent dragged me over and I stood there while Mick was deep in conversation with someone. I kept wanting to leave, but my agent insisted I stay. After about ten minutes, Mick's guest finally walked away and my agent introduced me and I stammered out a far too sober "H-hi, Mick," to which Mick said a very quick "Nice to meet you" and headed off into the crowd. (I'm not sure if the lesson from this story is to have a calming cocktail if you're nervous at a party or that the "I'll lurk next to you in your field of vision until you've finished talking" approach to meeting celebrities can ruin an otherwise good time you might have been having. I'll let you know when I figure it out.)

Laurie and I are known for throwing big parties in our backyard and inviting a lot of people I've worked with, including famous actors. I always stress about these parties because I want people to have a great time and am deathly afraid of being a lame host. I usually end up running around a lot, making sure I greet everyone and have a conversation with each and every person, which can be a bit stressful. But people always have such a good time seeing one another outside of work that I'm glad we throw these soirees, despite the occasional faux pas. Like the time I hugged Wendi McLendon-Covey with a glass of red wine in my hand and sloshed it all over the back of her very beautiful white blouse. I knew it had happened and was horrified. I also couldn't tell if she felt it, so I chose to not say anything about it, a decision I still cringe about to this day because *clearly* she knew it happened. I later saw her lovely husband trying to dab it off with a napkin. Wendi, I've never talked to you directly about this incident, but I would like to take this opportunity in writing to say I will never stop being sorry about doing that. Good lord.

Anywhooo . . .

So what should you do when it comes to throwing your party?

First, start small. It's your cocktail party, so you're going to be making the drinks. If you have one hundred people at your first cocktail party, you're not going to see anybody apart from asking them what they want to drink and handing

them the finished product. You'll be filling and refilling so many drink orders that you'll be living the cocktail party equivalent of the people who paint the Golden Gate Bridge—the minute they finish painting it, they immediately have to start painting it again because it's so freaking big. Even if everyone else has a great time, you'll end the evening feeling like the overworked waitstaff.

Starting your cocktail party hosting with a small group of the people you're most comfortable with will guarantee a fun time for both you and your guests. They'll get to talk to you and you'll get to enjoy them enjoying your cocktails. You'll have peace of mind knowing that everybody there will get along and that there won't be any lulls in the conversation. It'll just be a very fun, low-key hang. With cocktails!

Once you've done a few of those, you can graduate to a bigger cocktail party. The best larger gatherings I've been to were thrown by people I know who are just

as great at mixing and matching a disparate array of guests as they are at mixing cocktails. While you can always simply invite all your friends over for drinks, it's worth looking at your cocktail party the same way you look at your cocktails. You can play it safe with a tried-and-true recipe of your favorite ingredients that you know go together easily, or you can take a chance on a new recipe of ingredients that you know you like separately but never before thought of combining.

I'm lucky enough to have some amazing friends, like my pal the Australian novelist Kathy Lette, who are absolute masters at inviting guests to their cocktail parties who have nothing in common other than they're all interesting people. People from showbiz, scientists, doctors, architects, designers, poets, politicians, eccentrics—all people who wouldn't ordinarily meet in everyday life are suddenly at a party together, having been vetted and invited by their trusted host, and because they're all on the same common friendship ground they're able to approach one another safely and introduce themselves. From this comes fascinating discussions and new friendships as they learn about one another and what they do for a living and what they have in common. And it's all made easier and much more lively because of cocktails!

Cocktails can be the oil in the machine of social interactions. Sure, you don't need people to drink in order to meet and get along, but it does help in the loosening-up department a lot of the time. I know I'm weirdly shy when I walk into a room of people I don't know (or when I awkwardly meet Mick Jagger), so I have a hard time simply approaching other guests and introducing myself. But once I have a martini in my hand and few sips in my system, I'm suddenly a bit less shy. I lose that mental layer that says "Oh, they don't really want to meet me" or "You shouldn't bother them; they look like they're having a good enough time on their own" and find myself able to walk up and say hi. (And if you're Meryl Streep, odds are I'll come up and say hi *three times*!) When I think about the friendships I wouldn't have today because I'd have been too nervous to walk up and get to know them, I thank the heavens for whatever drink I happened to have in my hand at that moment that got me past my timidity.

Look, I know the downsides of drinking alcohol and am not pushing anyone to start relying on booze for strength and confidence. But as my father always said when I was growing up, "All things in moderation." It's important to drink responsibly, and there are plenty of people who have problems with addiction or can't handle their liquor or simply don't want to drink. You should always provide for nondrinkers at your cocktail party by having great nonalcoholic drinks on hand

so that everyone can have a refreshment while they socialize, and you should make sure those nonalcoholic drinks are presented as nicely and coolly as any alcoholic cocktail so that the nondrinkers don't feel like they're being treated any differently. (Don't just hand them a glass of club soda. Stick a lime or lemon wedge on the lip of the glass or hang a plastic monkey holding a cocktail cherry over the side. Having a nonalcoholic drink in your hand shouldn't be a scarlet letter.) It's also up to you to make sure no one at your party overdrinks and that anyone who has had drinks doesn't drive themselves home, either by ensuring there are designated drivers or by making sure that everyone has access to an Uber or Lyft, a cab, or some other type of public transportation. As the host, you are legally and morally responsible for your guests' safety, so you need to factor all that into your hosting duties.

But as long as you do things the right and responsible way, there's no reason why you and your friends can't enjoy a great evening of grown-up fun. And that's what cocktail parties are all about.

THE FOOD

Should you serve food at a cocktail party? Let me answer that for you.

Of course you should!!! Are you seriously going to booze people up on empty stomachs??? What are you, some kind of monster???!!!

Okay, now that I got that out of my system . . .

You'd be amazed at how many people don't know they need to put out food when they have you over for cocktails. If they don't invite you over for "dinner" and just for "drinks," there's a tendency for some hosts to think that it's literally

just drinks they're supposed to provide. But booze without food is not only a recipe for disaster— it's just kind of cruel. Even the diviest bar will put out peanuts or pretzels. Sure, they're trying to make you thirsty with salty snacks so that you'll order more drinks, but they also know you'll probably pass out if you have a couple of drinks with no food in your system.

You don't have to put out a full spread. Bowls of chips and popcorn are at least something. But you should pick a few appetizers that will both complement your drinks and get something to soak up the booze in your guests' stomachs. Cheese, hummus, olives, cold cuts, dips, pizza, those old-timey celery sticks with blue cheese spread in the indent, mini-meatballs—the list is endless. Just make sure to think about it and plan it out as carefully as you do your cocktail list. Because people always remember who served them food at a party and who hung them out to dry with booze and nothing to eat, no matter how nice they are or how happy they seemed at the party. The hangovers they'll wake up with the following morning will make them remember what a crappy host you were. Trust me.

One thing that will help you in the food department (as well as with all the other planning you're going to put into your cocktail party) is to come up with a theme. I don't mean it has to be like a bar mitzvah with a *Star Wars* or a *Harry Potter* theme. I just mean you should figure out what the overall unifying feel of the party is.

Are you going for a retro-vibe party with traditional cocktails like martinis and whiskey sodas? If so, look up appetizers from the 1950s and '60s, like canapés and fondue and those stuffed celery sticks I was just talking about. Maybe you want more of an Italian theme so that you can serve Negronis and Aperol spritzes. In

that case, you could do a nice assortment of Italian meats and cheeses. Or you may be in the mood to make tropical-themed drinks. In that case, you could go with mini-eggrolls and pineapple-chicken skewers.

Look, I'm no Martha Stewart. There are plenty of sources for advice on appetizers and easy-to-prepare snacks. I just know that the more you narrow down what your party is and what you want it to say to your guests, the less time you'll have to spend thinking up what food to serve. Take a stroll through your local grocery store's freezer section and see what appetizers you can pop in the oven and put out on a tray. Even if it's just frozen mini-pizzas that you picked up at your local convenience store, people will appreciate it because you took the time to do it. If an appetizer is hot, you'll get bonus points because they'll see you put some extra effort into it. Sure, you can work your way up to really impressive and more expensive gourmet goodies in time, but for the purposes of just getting into the cocktail game, if you put out food that you thought about and paired to your cocktails, people will come to your next party, and the party after that. (Assuming you want them back!)

THE MUSIC

Music is as essential to a cocktail party as are the cocktails themselves. Once again, it's your party, so the choice is up to you. Pick the music that will make you happy and that you think will make your guests happy. Put together a playlist so you can just switch it on and not think about it again until the party is over, or simply put on one of the myriad playlists available on any of the streaming music services, like Spotify. Old music, new music, classical music, dance music, cocktail music, jazz—whatever you think will complement the vibe you're trying to create for your party.

That said, I personally have one rule I go by when it comes to music, and that is to not blast it so loud that your guests have to shout at one another to be heard. While it's true you want the music to be present, not just haunting around like a whispery ghost in the deep background, turning your cocktail party into a rock concert or rave isn't the best way to create

the social interaction that is the real purpose of a cocktail party in the first place.

Nobody loves music more than I do. And I love my music loud. When I'm in the car, I play it so loud, sometimes I worry I'm going to get pulled over by the cops. But when I'm in a restaurant or at a party and the music is blaring and competing with a conversation I'm trying to have, it's really irritating. I get in a bad mood when I have to strain to hear people, or when they can't hear me and I need to repeat the pithy comment I just fired off.

In short, a cocktail party isn't a *party* party. A flat-out party is all about dancing and raucous good times and people cutting loose. A cocktail party is about mingling, about good conversation and getting to know people better. It's about unwinding and making others laugh and learning about new things, about exchanging ideas and opinions and relaxing. And it's hard to do that when you're competing with whatever music is playing. In short, your music should provide the backbeat to your party, not overtake it like some attention-hungry soloist. (When I was in my late

teens in Detroit, I was dating a girl who made me take her to a Triumph concert at Cobo Hall. I wasn't a fan of the band and the concert was too long and the guitar player did a twenty-minute meandering but earsplitting guitar solo and I was so aggravated by it all that my girlfriend and I ended up breaking up on the way home. Don't let your music be like the guitar player in Triumph when you throw a party is what I'm trying to say.)

Beyond that, you are free to create whatever atmosphere you want with the music you play. I like to make my party feel more old-timey adult by putting on music by Xavier Cugat, Esquivel, Frank Sinatra, and Dean Martin and genres like bossa nova, Brazilian beat, and classic jazz. But any music is fine and fun if it's there as a nice background to your get-together. Judge it all by the crowd you invite and stay aware of it as the party progresses. Sometimes you'll find you want to turn the music up a bit to get some more energy if the party is starting to flag. Other times you'll want to turn it down as the conversation heats up and more people join into bigger discussions. A cocktail party has a true ebb and flow, and if you're the one at the helm keeping things moving effectively, your party is only going to be the better for it.

MUSIC TO MAKE COCKTAILS BY

In the recipes that follow, I have paired each cocktail with its own song. Why, you ask? Well, I think that making a cocktail should be just as fun as drinking it, and so the mixing of your libation doesn't have to be some silent chore. I always like to put something on my speakers to celebrate the fact that I'm about to have a much-deserved drink. (Whether I actually deserve it is another question. But who am I to judge myself? Um . . . moving on.)

The point is—have fun while you create. Celebrate the moment of mixology. As Madonna once sang, let your body move to the music. If it's a shaken cocktail, then a great song gives you the backbeat to inspire your shaker skills. Cocktail time is your time, so make it joyous. Because you'll just be back to normal life tomorrow.

THE DRESS CODE

Your cocktail party is a chance to step things up for yourself and your guests. Sure, everybody enjoys being comfortable, but a cocktail party allows you to go to the next level, to put on something nice and look your best both for yourself and for the people you're going to meet. In what I refer to today as the Tyranny of the Casual, there seems to be a feeling that we have to be comfortable at all costs, no matter where we are. I'm old enough to have gone to Las Vegas when people actually wore suits and gowns and tuxedoes in the casinos, bars, and restaurants. These days,

Laurie and I have eaten in three-star Vegas restaurants while seated next to guys in shorts, baseball hats, and Tweety Bird T-shirts. Of course you can have an overly comfortable, super-casual cocktail party if you want to. But, if I may ask without sounding too obnoxious, why would you?

Cocktail culture is all about being an adult and enjoying grown-up things. Dressing nicely is a part of that. It's little kids and teens who have to be forced to put on their "good clothes," not anyone in their twenties and beyond. Or at least it shouldn't be. Once you're an adult, you should leave that "I don't want to get dressed up!" part of yourself behind, along with not eating your vegetables and believing that the world is fair. Lounging around at a party in your tank top and sweatpants slurping cocktails sort of defeats the whole purpose of the event. You and your friends could do that anytime. Let's make our cocktail parties special!

The most important thing is to let your guests know what you expect them to wear. It's annoying to get an invite to a party and there's no indication of what

the host expects people to put on, and so you arrive either way too overdressed or way too underdressed. (For the record, I personally feel you can never be too overdressed. Then again, wearing white tie and tails to a pool party might be a bit much. Although I may or may not have done that on a few occasions.) So you should always let people know if the party is super-casual, casual, business attire, cocktail attire, or black tie/formal. Let them in on the theme of the party, too, if you have one. Your guests may want to give a little nod to whatever it is you're highlighting at the party, like wearing a certain style of suit or dress or adding some sort of fun and/or funny brooch or other adornment to their outfits. My mom used to have a pin or necklace for every holiday, as well as some that were just evocative of certain times of the year, like autumn leaves or spring blooms. The more info you give your guests, the more fun they'll have planning their outfits so they can bring their maximum personality to the party, if that's their thing.

My dream—one I've still never made happen—is to have a formal black-tie cocktail party at our house. I would hire a jazz trio and require that all the men wear tuxedoes and all the women wear whatever kind of formal outfit they feel the most elegant in, whether it's a gown or a suit or a tuxedo of their own. We'd have the same kind of fun conversation and music and laughs that we do at our more informal parties, but it would add that extra touch of grown-up class to the proceedings.

But I haven't done it yet, partly because I never want to make somebody who doesn't have formal wear feel bad, and I don't cherish the idea of someone having to go to a tuxedo rental store as if they're getting ready for the prom. As a friend of mine says about rental tuxedoes, "I don't want to wear something that a teenager probably had sex in." So my dream of a formal cocktail party remains unrealized. But let's make a vow right here and now that we will all work toward that goal. Just make sure to take a lot of pictures when you do!

Cocktail parties are all about mingling and conversation. But what if you want to kick your soiree into high gear and still keep it interactive? Well, if you play the piano or guitar, there's nothing that ups the fun more than a good old-fashioned sing-along. Just make sure that it's actually a sing-along and not a showcase for your solo singing-and-songwriting career. In other words, don't turn your guests into your audience. If you start playing well-known songs that everybody likes, the whole gang will jump in and start singing along. Pop hits, classics, show tunes—tailor the playlist to the interests of your guests and watch them have the time of their lives. Throw in a basket of maracas for the non-singers in the crowd and no one will feel left out.

Don't play an instrument that can carry a tune? No problem! Do what my friend Steve Higgins and his family do—have a playlist showdown. Hook guests' phones into whatever sound system you have at your party and let people take turns surprising each other with their favorite party songs. The only rule is anybody can change the song after a minute. (Unless someone picks a real stinker. Then let the knives come out!) Dancing, laughter, and good times are guaranteed!

LOOKING FOR MORE FUN?

THE DRINKS!

Okay, we've talked about what you need to prepare cocktails and we've talked about how to best let you and your friends enjoy them. But now it's time for the fun part—the actual drinks and how to make them!

In addition to the recipes, as I stated earlier, I've included a song that I think goes well with each cocktail. Take my advice or pick your own soundtrack. The key is to have fun making each cocktail and even more fun drinking it. It's all part of the experience.

And away we go!

THE COCKTAIL 100

COCKTAIL #1—THE MARTINI!

THE KING OF COCKTAILS

The song—"One Mint Julep" by Xavier Cugat

I'll admit it. The martini is my favorite cocktail in the world. I'll also admit I'm prejudiced—prejudiced against vodka martinis. Not that they aren't good. It's just that most people these days seem to think a vodka martini is a real martini. No, I'm not trying to be a judgmental asshole when I say that, although clearly I'm making a judgment and do sort of sound like an asshole. I'm just tired of people asking "Vodka or gin?" when I say I love martinis, because a gin martini is the true martini.

When you order a martini, the bartender should automatically use gin. If you order a vodka martini, then, sure, they can use vodka and you can enjoy it.

But a real martini is made with gin. End of story. So there. Nyah.

What a judgmental asshole I am.

Now that we've pushed past that bit of unpleasantness, let's talk about the best way to make a martini. The truth is there's really no definitive method, although any martini aficionado (i.e., *me*) will have a very strong opinion about that. But I'm flexible and reasonable enough to admit that the perfect martini is all about your own personal taste.

Some people like their martinis very dry. Others like them "wetter," with more vermouth. Some like a twist of lemon. Some like olives. Some like olives so much that they like their martinis dirty. Some like them *very* dirty, so that they look like swamp water. Some like them shaken. Others like them stirred. There are many ways to make a martini, although we all reserve the right to think that the way you like them isn't nearly as good as the way *we* like them.

Gins are the snowflakes of booze—no two are alike and there's an infinite number of them. The more juniper there is, the sharper and more challenging the gin will taste. The lighter ones are probably better if you're transitioning from vodka.

Fundamentally, gin is really just vodka (an ethanol/water mix) flavored with botanicals. How these botanicals affect the taste of the gin is all about what is known in the gin world as "the basket."

When gin is distilled, the ethanol is put into a still, then a basket of botanicals is dropped in with it. It's easiest to think of the basket as a big tea bag. Various herbs, spices, and fruit by-products are stacked in the basket and infused into the ethanol as the gin is distilled. But the kinds of botanicals that can be put into the basket are endless.

WHICH GIN IS RIGHT FOR YOU?

First and foremost are juniper berries. Without juniper berries, gin simply isn't gin. It's about the only consistent flavor in gin. But the amount and prevalence of the juniper can be varied endlessly. Some gins, especially the older brands, are very juniper-forward. This results in the pine tree smell and taste that has put so many people off gin in the past. Many of us at one point in our youth snuck down to a friend's parents' basement bar or liquor cabinet, pulled out a bottle of gin, took a swig, and gagged at the blast of Pine-Sol cleanser taste, vowing never to drink gin again. At least I know that happened to me when I was nine in the basement of one of my parents' bridge club friends. The perils of underage drinking.

But today there are so many different combinations of botanicals in the endless number of gins on the market that it's possible to never encounter that pine forest taste again. Various citrus peels, spices ranging from black pepper to peppermint, savory ingredients like rosemary and thyme, and all the flavors in between are now fair game to find their place in the basket.

In addition, the order the botanicals are stacked in the basket affects how they are infused into the ethanol, which creates further variations. Then the alcohol percentage affects *those* variations. When I was working on the recipe for my Artingstall's Brilliant London Dry Gin, the difference between the exact same basket formula at 40 percent, 42 percent, and 44 percent alcohol content was amazingly varied. At 40 percent, the botanicals came too far forward on the palate and made the gin too herbal. At 44 percent, the flavors were hidden by the alcohol taste and the gin was too harsh. At 42 percent, we had the perfect balance of booze and botanicals.

So how do you pick your favorite? Well, there's no surefire way other than to try different ones and see what you like. Ask a bartender or a gin-loving friend for their recommendations. They'll most likely ask you if you like your gin super ginny or if you like ones that are milder. Have them pour you a very juniper-forward one (such as Beefeater, Junipero, Berry Bros & Rudd "#3") and something lighter (such as Artingstall's, Hendrick's, Oxley) and see what you respond to. Just avoid any flavored or fruity ones when it comes to martinis. Those are great in other cocktails, but a martini needs to taste like gin. The right one is out there, filled with enough botanical flavor to make your martini the perfect drink for you. Get tasting and find your gin, my friend. What research could be more fun than that?

I think the snobbery around martinis comes from the fact that the differences between variations are so incremental. You're working with only three ingredients, and frankly, one of the ingredients is basically an add-on. Dropping an olive in or squeezing a twist over the surface of a martini certainly changes the shape and taste of it, but it's the relationship between the gin (or vodka, if you must) and the vermouth that is where the real science comes in.

In the old days, martinis used to be very "wet," for lack of a better term. They tended to be equal parts gin and vermouth. But as time went by, martinis got drier and drier. Legend has it that Winston Churchill liked his martinis so dry that his advice was to pour the gin into the glass and then look across the room at the bottle of vermouth. (All due respect to Mr. Churchill, but that isn't really a martini—it's just a bunch of gin in a martini glass.) But the vermouth is there to open things up, to round the drink out a bit, to take it away from being simply one type of alcohol with a garnish floating in it. And that combination is where the magic—and mistakes— happen.

Here I give you three ways to make a basic martini. They're in descending order of my preference, but I'd happily drink any of them if a bartender made one for me. These are all considered very dry martinis. You can use these same methods to experiment with more vermouth, if you'd like. At the end of the day, it's all about personal taste.

THE GOLD STANDARD
THE DUKES BAR MARTINI

About 3½ ounces gin (the size of your glass will decide this)

A little bit of vermouth

Large twist of lemon

This is the famous martini they make at Dukes Bar in London, which is in Dukes Hotel, a small hidden gem off St. James's. The Dukes martini was invented because a martini must be very cold to be good. In the quest for the coldest martini possible, Salvatore Calabrese first came up with this method in the mid-1980s. But it was my good friend and bartender extraordinaire Alessandro Palazzi, the head bartender at Dukes since the mid-1990s, who perfected it and made it come to life.

IT'S really quite simple. Unbelievably simple, actually. But it requires prep. First, put a bottle of your favorite gin and a martini glass into the freezer several hours before you plan on making your drink. When the gin is ice-cold through and through, take the glass and gin out of the freezer and immediately pour a small amount of vermouth into the glass. The vermouth doesn't have to be cold, although it can be. If it's not, the frozen gin will be cold enough to make up for it.

NEXT, turn the glass with it tipped at an angle so the vermouth coats the walls of the glass as you slowly spin it one full revolution. Then, discard the rest of the vermouth from the glass into the sink or, if you want to be like Alessandro, dump it out onto the carpet. (This is Alessandro's signature move, which he pioneered. If you do it, it is required that you say "Thank you, Alessandro" each time, in honor of him.)

NOW, before the glass has a chance to defrost, pour in the frozen gin. Fill the glass right to the top, leaving just enough space that you don't spill all over the place when you pick up your drink. (Although when Alessandro makes a martini, he can fill it right to the very rim and set the glass down in front of you without spilling a drop. The man has the steadiest hand in London.)

NEXT, take a good-size lemon and, using a very sharp knife or vegetable peeler, cut off a long piece of peel, otherwise known as a twist. (You want to make sure the twist isn't too thick. If it is, when you squeeze it in the next step it will snap in half, which you don't want.) If the lemon is big, you can cut the twist pole to pole. If it's a smaller one, go around the circumference so that you can make the twist longer. The perfect twist tends to be 2 to 3 inches long, although there are no points off for making it even longer. What you don't want is a weeny little twist that simply floats on top of your martini. A good twist sits with one end on the bottom of the glass and the other end sticking up a good ½ to 1 inch out of the martini, like a porpoise asking for a fish at SeaWorld. (Those little thin pigtail-shaped ones some bars put in martinis are worthless. The whole point of a twist is to add lemon oil to your drink. It shouldn't just look like a yellow pubic hair is floating in your martini.)

SQUEEZE the twist over the surface of the martini. Now, when I say squeeze it, I mean grip it on its edges, aiming the skin side at the surface of the drink, and squeezing so that it folds almost in half lengthwise and releases a spray of oil onto the surface of the martini. If you look closely, you'll see little shiny spots on top of the drink, much like oil on the surface of a puddle. This means you've done it correctly.

TAKE the skin side of the twist, which will now be wet with oil, and rub it around the rim of the glass to coat the edges with the rest of the oil. This way, when you take a drink, you'll get a bit of extra lemon taste.

NOW put the twist into the drink, carefully pick the glass up, and taste the world's greatest, coldest, most elegant martini.

A note of caution: What you are now drinking is basically straight gin. It has not touched ice. It has not been diluted. It has not been watered down by more than a drop of vermouth. It is straight alcohol. So it packs a wallop, especially if you're using a higher-alcohol gin. (I personally like to use gin with an alcohol content between 40 and 44 percent for my martinis; the gin I make, Artingstall's, is a friendly 42 percent. Anything stronger and your evening may end much earlier than you wanted it to.) At Dukes, Alessandro will cut you off at two martinis, no matter who you are. I was there one time when a couple of businessmen were having a sober-seeming conversation for an hour and then one got up to go to the restroom and fell flat on his face. Alessandro ran up to the other bartender who had been serving them and asked, "How many did you serve him?" and the bartender said, "Three," to which Alessandro barked, "Never three! No more than two!"

THIS brings me to another important point, one that I alluded to back in our glassware section, something I have a very strong opinion about—glass size. In the old days of the infamous three-martini lunches, martinis tended to be about 1½ ounces. They came in small, stemmed glasses and were pretty easy to toss back. Martinis then started to get bigger, with a 4-ounce glass becoming the norm. But in the last few decades, the Big Gulp ethos seems to have infected the bars of our world and the 10-ounce martini has become the norm.

LET me state it clearly: A 10-ounce martini is ridiculous. First of all, it's so big that unless you down it quickly, it will be warm when there's still half of it left. And second, a 10-ounce martini means that you're drinking over one third of a bottle of gin in a single cocktail. A martini is meant to start the evening before you go on to dinner and enjoy a few glasses of wine or another cocktail with your meal. If you down more than a third of a bottle of gin before you've even eaten, unless you're Superman, you're really setting yourself up for a fall.

A 4-ounce martini is the perfect size. You can nurse it as you talk with your friends and it will remain cold. You'll finish it feeling nicely relaxed and ready for a fun evening. And, hopefully, you won't be roaring drunk at the end of a meal that includes wine and an after-dinner drink. A giant martini at the beginning of the evening is the equivalent of building your house on sand. No, reject the 10-ounce martini, my friend. It is the very definition of more is less. Keep it classy! And stay conscious!

THE RUNNER-UP
THE STIRRED MARTINI

Ice

About
3½ ounces gin

Dash of vermouth

Large twist of
lemon

James Bond is famous for always wanting his martinis "shaken, not stirred." I've puzzled about this for years. I've always considered James Bond the epitome of cool, and yet I find the shaken martini to be much less cool for several reasons. First, it waters down the gin. Second, it creates a flotilla of ice chips on top of your drink if it's shaken vigorously enough. And third, it makes the martini so cloudy that it arrives looking a bit like a glass of dirty dishwater.

But then I realized something. James Bond is an international superspy who needs to always be alert and ready for action. By having his martini shaken, he may *want* it to be watered down so that it doesn't hit him as hard and he can still have all (or most) of his wits about him. So I now give Mr. Bond a free pass on his shaken request.

For those of us who aren't international superspies, however, a stirred martini is the way to go if you're not going to do the full-on Dukes treatment. Quite frankly, a stirred martini is probably the safest martini to have. You get some subtle dilution of the gin from the ice, you get the pageantry of watching a bartender swirl your drink around in a nice glass mixing pitcher with a long, elegant bar spoon as they get the drink ice cold, and you have fun watching them put a strainer on top of the mixing pitcher and pour the beautiful, clear drink into a chilled martini glass.

IT'S simple to make. First, chill a martini glass in the freezer or pour ice into a room-temperature one to get it nice and cold. Now, get a mixing glass or large clear tumbler if you have one, or use the bottom half of your metal shaker if you don't. Fill it with ice (don't skimp on the ice—stirring a martini with just a few ice cubes won't get it cold enough and will cause the ice to melt more quickly, thus watering down the martini more than it needs to be). Put in a quick dash of vermouth, then add the gin. Use a long mixing spoon (or a regular spoon or a thin knife or even a chopstick if it's all you have) to stir the martini briskly for 1 to 2 minutes. Again, you want to get this drink ice-cold. I've been in bars where they only stir it for about 15 seconds and serve me a lukewarm martini that I then send back to be stirred with ice again for a couple of minutes. A warm martini is a bad martini.

GRAB your chilled martini glass (throw out the ice if you're chilling the glass that way) and strain the martini into the glass. Cut and squeeze the twist over it as described in the Dukes Bar Martini (page 58). Sip and enjoy!

HONORABLE MENTION
THE SHAKEN MARTINI

Ice

About
3½ ounces gin

Dash of vermouth

Large twist of
lemon

As I mentioned in the previous recipe, I'm not a huge fan of the shaken martini. But it has its place in your repertoire because that's the way a lot of people want it. The biggest advantage is that there are few things cooler than shaking a cocktail shaker. It is the heart and soul of mixology. I'm a fan of many other cocktails, and the vast majority of them are shaken. To see a great bartender manipulate a shaker with real artistry and flair is to be in the presence of an amazing performer. The sound of ice in a shaker has a music to it that makes any cocktail aficionado's mouth water. It's a key part of the pageantry of cocktail making, the step that everyone understands. It *is* mixology. And it's okay to embrace it.

The other good thing about a shaken martini is the fact that it waters the gin down more, which really gives you a fighting chance in these days of the 10-ounce martini. A sea of ice chips atop a fairly watery martini means that it's both very cold and also not as much of an ass-kicking monster that it would be if you Dukes-ed it. When I'm in a place where the only martini option is the big 10-ouncer, I'll usually just let them shake the hell out of it and try to drink only half. (And when I do make it all the way through one of those giants, which is more often than I care to admit, I'm usually . . . well . . . okay, I was going to fudge and say the room isn't spinning, but 10 ounces of watery, ice-topped gin is still 10 ounces of gin!)

Anyway, all judgments aside, here are the extremely simple directions for making a shaken martini.

FILL your shaker about two-thirds full of ice. Put in a dash of vermouth and the gin and shake for 1 to 2 minutes. What you don't have to do is shake it like a maniac. The harder you shake, the more you chip and break up the ice. If you want a ton of ice chips in your martini, then shake your brains out. I'm not here to judge. But if you want to keep it in the world of a proper martini, then a good rhythmic but reserved shake is fine.

NEXT, either strain the martini into a chilled glass through the opening at the top of the cobbler shaker or remove the full top and use a cocktail strainer to pour it. Do the twist as described in the Dukes Bar Martini (page 58) and sip away.

OTHER "MARTINIS"

There are a million recipes for all flavors and forms of other martinis—apple, chocolate, espresso, mango, pineapple—the list goes on forever. And many of these are really fun and tasty. Just keep in mind that to the true martini aficionado, these are just inventive cocktails that happen to come in large martini-shaped glasses. Only gin with a bit of vermouth and however you want to garnish it is a true martini.

COCKTAIL #2—THE NEGRONI

KING OF ITALIAN COCKTAILS

The song—"Groove Is in the Heart" by Deee-Lite

Ice

1 ounce gin

1 ounce sweet vermouth

1 ounce Campari or any other bitter red Italian aperitivo

Orange twist or slice

What is so damn good about a Negroni is what I would call its simple complexity. It's a very easy-to-make drink consisting of three ingredients in equal amounts—gin, sweet vermouth, and Italian bitter liqueur—poured directly into a glass, then stirred and topped with an orange twist. But it is the complexity of the way these three ingredients interact with and affect one another that makes a Negroni one of the kings of the mixed drinks.

Even though the three basic ingredients of a Negroni are fairly set in stone, with slight variations there are infinite possibilities, and it's possible to never make the same Negroni twice.

The building block of this drink is the gin. As discussed (see page 52), there are countless varieties of gin, distinguished by the botanicals used and their proportions, the order they're stacked in the basket, and the alcohol percentage. The kind of gin you pick affects the taste of your Negroni, and the best gin for your Negroni may not be the same one you like in your martini. In a Negroni, since the gin is contending with two other very pushy ingredients, you may want a bolder gin taste to make it stand out. Play with different brands each time you mix one up, if possible.

The next ingredient brings the sweetness. Sweet vermouth has many subtle (and sometimes not so subtle) variations in its taste. The standard Martini & Rossi/ Noilly Prat/Dolin sweet vermouths that we find in most bars tend to be on the sweeter and less complex side. They work perfectly and don't really compete too heavily with the gin. They provide the sweet quality that is one of the essential parts of a Negroni, which is the perfect meeting of sweet, bitter, and alcohol flavors.

However, there are other types of sweet vermouth that can add even more complexity. (And sometimes compete with the gin and bitter in a bad way. You never know.) Slightly spicier and more fortified sweet vermouths, like Antica Formula and Martini Riserva Speciale Rubino, can supply a kick of zing as well as a bit of extra bitterness mixed in with the sweet.

This leads us to the bitter. The Italian red bitter liqueur you use can bring along even more variations to the mix. The traditional bitter in a Negroni is Campari, but I personally find it to be a bit too sweet and syrupy. There are other bitter red liqueur alternatives coming out of Italy that offer their own extra infusion of spice. The good folks at Galliano make a bitter aperitivo that adds even more spice along with the bitterness but none of the sweetness. Martini, Luxardo, Tempus Fugit, and Nardini, among others, also make red bitters with their own distinct qualities.

So, with all these considerations, our simple and elegant Negroni quickly becomes something much less simple but much more interesting. Whatever versions of these ingredients you use (and it's definitely worth experimenting with different ones to find your favorite formula), it's still a knockout of a drink.

PUT ice into an old fashioned glass, then add the gin, sweet vermouth, and red bitter aperitivo directly into the glass. Stir with a cocktail spoon or swizzle stick to combine the ingredients and get them nice and cold. Add a sizable orange twist to the drink. (You can squeeze the twist over the top of the Negroni if you want to add a bit more orange flavor from the oil of the skin, which will really bring out the extra tastes of the drink.) Or, instead of the twist, you can just drop in a whole slice of orange. Up to you! Then take a sip and relax as you savor the sweet and bitter flavors uniting on your tongue. *Cento di questi giorni!*

VARIATIONS

APEROL NEGRONI

Laurie isn't a huge fan of red bitter liqueurs, so for her I tend to replace the Campari with Aperol, an orange-flavored aperitivo liqueur that's best known for being the key ingredient in an Aperol Spritz (page 69). Laurie and I discovered this drink back in the 1990s when we first started going to Italy on vacation. In Venice, we noticed that most Italians had an Aperol Spritz before they went out to dinner. We used to smuggle home bottles of Aperol in our suitcases because it wasn't available in the United States, but it's now become as ubiquitous here as Campari.

SUBSTITUTING Aperol for Campari makes the Negroni a much sweeter drink. Because of this, many Negroni purists don't consider it to be a true Negroni, and they are right. A true Negroni is all about the interplay between the tastes of the bittersweet Campari and sweet vermouth. But if you don't like bitter flavors, a Negroni with Aperol might just be the drink for you.

SELECT NEGRONI

Select is another red bitter liqueur, but it falls comfortably between Campari and Aperol in the bitter-versus-sweet realm. Laurie and I discovered it in Venice in the early 2010s. We were at Osteria Da Fiore for dinner, and Laurie was trying to figure out what drink she wanted to start with. I suggested a Negroni, which she rejected as being too bitter, and then I said, "Why not do it with Aperol?" But that night she felt it would be too sweet for what she was craving. The waiter suggested, "What about Select?" We had no idea what he was talking about, but he said he would make her a Negroni with it, and it was absolutely delicious. He told us that Select was an aperitivo available only in Venice. He showed us the bottle, which had a drawing of the front of a gondola on the label. Once again, we smuggled several bottles back in our suitcases. But Select is starting to become more available outside of Italy, and any good liquor store should have it these days.

THE main taste in Select is basically berries, and many people might not even be able to pinpoint the difference between a Negroni made with Campari and one made with Select, but they would definitely feel less of a bitter edge. There's just a lovely smoothness to a Select Negroni that I highly recommend. If you're lucky enough to come across a bottle, give it a try. Just substitute Select for the Campari. Easy-peasy!

DUBONNET NEGRONI

You can also substitute Dubonnet Rouge for the sweet vermouth. I'll explain more about Dubonnet on page 77, but it will give the sweet component of your Negroni a bit more of a spicy edge. It's worth a try!

NEGRONI SBAGLIATO

The Negroni Sbagliato is another great version. *Sbagliato* basically means "mistake," but what a delicious mistake it is. My good friend Wei Koh, owner of *The Rake* magazine and one of the most tasteful men I know, first turned me on to these.

A NEGRONI SBAGLIATO is simply a Negroni made with prosecco instead of gin. While it makes the Negroni a tad sweeter, it also has the benefit of letting you have an extra Negroni or two before you get to the same alcoholic content of one traditional gin-based Negroni. It's a perfect and tasty way to keep your evening from getting too boozy too fast. I highly recommend you try one of these sometime. You won't regret it!

WHITE NEGRONI

With a couple of different ingredients, you can make a White Negroni that's both delicious and not too far off from a traditional dark Negroni. Suze is a clear, almost yellow bitter liqueur from France. It's very similar in taste to Campari, but I would dare say it's even a little more bitter than its red Italian cousin. Lillet Blanc is a sweet apéritif wine that works as a worthy clearer substitute for the red sweet vermouths. A clear dry vermouth wouldn't be sweet enough to counteract the bitterness of the Suze, so Lillet Blanc is the perfect counterpart.

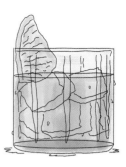

Ice

1 ounce gin

1 ounce Lillet Blanc apéritif

1 ounce Suze gentian liqueur

Orange twist

STIR the ingredients in an old fashioned glass with ice the same way you would a regular Negroni. Add the twist of orange and enjoy a drink that not a lot of people know about! *Très chic!*

TREAT YOUR VERMOUTH RIGHT

I can't tell you how many times I've been at someone's house and asked if they have vermouth only to have them pull out some ancient half-filled bottle of it from the back of their cupboard. Vermouth is basically wine, and we all know that wine goes bad pretty quickly once you open it. Vermouth is no exception. You have to refrigerate vermouth after you open it. Then it will last for several months. Old warm vermouth is no longer vermouth—it's vinegar. And not good vinegar. Treat your vermouth right and it will treat your cocktails right. Trust me.

COCKTAIL #3—THE SPRITZ!
THE PERFECT WAY TO START YOUR EVENING
The song—"We Are Family" by Sister Sledge

Ice

Aperol

Prosecco

Club soda (optional)

Orange slice or twist

There are few things more refreshing and fun than having a spritz at the start of your evening. As I've mentioned, Laurie and I first discovered spritzes in Venice in the '90s. The great thing about a spritz is that it helps transition you from day to night and serves as the warm-up act to whatever cocktail and/or wine you're planning to have with dinner and beyond. Spritzes are best enjoyed with potato chips, peanuts, and olives, the standard spritz accompaniments in Italy.

There are tons of ways to make spritzes, so I'll just tell you about Laurie's and my favorites. But there's really no right or wrong. The biggest variable is the ratio of aperitivo to prosecco and/or soda water. Some people like their spritzes on the sweeter side, while others like them much drier. Laurie likes hers quite dry, so I mix less aperitivo into her prosecco. I don't mind a little extra flavor, so tend to give myself more aperitivo. Your tastes are your own, and as long as you enjoy the final product, your spritz can be deemed a roaring success!

SINCE the Aperol Spritz is the most popular of the spritzes, I'll tell you how to make that one first. You'll notice that I don't include measurements here, as spritzes come in all shapes and sizes; of all the drinks in mixology, the spritz is probably the one that is most measured with the eye as opposed to the jigger.

IN Italy, I've had spritzes served in small highball glasses and in large wineglasses. Both are great. It depends on how big of a drink you want and how much ice you want in your spritz.

WHICHEVER size glass you use, first put in your ice. How much room the ice takes in your glass determines how much of the other ingredients you'll need. I recommend putting in enough ice to fill your glass three-quarters full. Spritzes are best when they're cold, so more ice is a good thing. A lukewarm spritz is a sad spritz.

NEXT, pour in the Aperol. I would suggest pouring in enough to put about a half inch of the aperitivo in the bottom of the glass. Once that's in, *slowly* pour in your prosecco. I don't know the scientific explanation for why this happens, but if you pour too fast, the ice makes the prosecco foam up and it can easily overflow the glass. Also, you want to pour slowly so you can watch the color of the drink.

SIMPLY put, the less orange the drink becomes, the lighter the Aperol taste will be and the less sweet the spritz will be. When you've filled the glass about three quarters full, give it a quick stir and take a sip. If you feel like you want more orange taste, add some more Aperol. If it seems fine, continue to pour in more prosecco. It's all about what tastes the best to you.

NOW, some bars top off their spritzes with a bit of club soda and others don't. Again, this is a personal taste issue. Adding a bit of soda water gives the drink some extra fizz, as well as bringing the intensity of the prosecco and Aperol down a bit. If you prefer a stronger-tasting drink, skip the club soda. If you want a bit more effervescence, go for the soda, especially if your prosecco isn't as fresh and bubbly as it could be. (If you order a spritz in a bar and don't see them open a fresh bottle of prosecco, I would recommend having them top your drink with some club soda. You never know how long that bottle they pull the stopper out of has been open.)

THE one thing you want to make certain of is that you're putting in very carbonated club soda. If it's not fizzy, you're just watering your spritz down. Lately I've found a lot of fancy sparkling waters with the most anemic bubbles I've ever seen. You don't want your club soda to be like water a baby farted in. Club soda should be lively. It should fizz and bubble up when you pour it into any drink or glass. I would steer you away from adding sparkling mineral waters like Pellegrino or Badoit, which tend toward calmness. Go for some good old club soda or seltzer water or, better yet, get yourself a SodaStream and make your own. This way, you can control exactly how bubbly your soda water is. My friend Steve Higgins and I practically run out the gas canister every time we make club soda, because we like very bubbly water. I've had the cap shoot off when I unscrew the bottle hours later because there's so much carbonation trapped inside. I guess I just have a bubbly personality. Pow! Comedy!

ANYWAY, if you're going to add club soda, go for the bubbles.

AFTER that, you can cut a slice of orange, chop it in half, and put it into your spritz. Give the whole concoction one more quick stir and pretend you're on vacation on the Italian Riviera.

VARIATIONS

CAMPARI SPRITZ

Substitute Campari for the Aperol for a bitter bubbly spritz!

LIMONCELLO SPRITZ

Limoncello is a great but deceptively strong lemon drink that waiters will bring you for free at the end of your meal in Italy if you've been a nice customer. It's basically grain alcohol infused with lemons and sugar. So it packs a punch. But it's also great in a spritz.

THE basic formula for a limoncello spritz is 3 parts prosecco, 2 parts limoncello, and 1 part soda water. Again, you can adjust this to your tastes, but it's a good ratio to follow. Just remember—a limoncello spritz will sneak up on you. On a hot day, it'll be tempting to have two or three. But when you stand up, you'll quickly remember that this was not your grandma's spritz. Spritz responsibly!!!

AND OF COURSE THERE'S ALWAYS GIN!

You can also add a splash or two of gin to any spritz to give it a little extra flavor and punch. There's no points off for doing that!

COCKTAIL #4—THE VESPER
THE DRINK JAMES BOND INVENTED

The song—"Jump Around" by House of Pain

Ice

3 ounces gin

1 ounce vodka

½ ounce Lillet Blanc apéritif

Lemon twist

In Ian Fleming's very first James Bond novel, *Casino Royale*, James falls in love with a woman by the name of Vesper. *Spoiler alert*—she's a double agent! Okay, now that I ruined that for you, I'll make it up to you by telling you that at the height of his love for her (before he knows that she's a . . . well . . . what I just said), James Bond invented a drink in her honor named, of course, the Vesper.

Since Mr. Bond is a lover of martinis, he had the decency to make her drink a variation on the martini by adding two more liquors to it. Well, one liquor and one liqueur. (Okay, technically Lillet is an apéritif, but I consider it a liqueur since it's a wine with liqueur and flavoring added to it and it functions like a liqueur in this recipe. So humor me and call it a liqueur, too.)

What's the difference between a liquor and a liqueur? A liqueur is a liquor (distilled spirit) that has been sweetened with oils, extracts, and flavors. Liquor is usually the base for a liqueur, but once a liquor has become a liqueur, it can't go back to being a liquor. Although liqueur is still liquor. Because it's all alcohol, really.

Confused? You bet you are. Think of it this way: Liquor is strong and liqueur is sweet. But still strong. But still not usually as strong as liquor. You're confused again, right? Well, make yourself a Vesper and you won't care anymore.

COMBINE the gin, vodka, and Lillet in a mixing glass or shaker with ice and either stir or shake, depending on how much dilution you want. (Remember, shaking with ice puts more water into the drink than stirring.) Strain into a chilled cocktail glass and squeeze the lemon twist over the surface of the drink to release the oil. Brush the rim of the glass with the twist and drop into the drink. Sip and savor the world, James Bond style! Double 0 delicious!

COCKTAIL #5—THE MANHATTAN

THE DRINK NEW YORK CITY LOVES SO MUCH IT LENT IT ITS NAME

The Song—"I'm Outta Love" by Anastacia

I resisted trying a Manhattan for a long time. Why? Well, I used to get it mixed up on the menu with a Cosmopolitan because (follow my logic here) Manhattan is a cosmopolitan place, and I didn't know what either drink really looked like. Then when I finally saw one, I decided a Manhattan just looked like a dark martini with a cherry in it; since I'm such a martini purist, I stuck to my beautiful clear martinis. Then, when I investigated further and saw that it was a whiskey-based drink, as a single-malt enthusiast I didn't want to waste a good pour of scotch.

Well, how wrong I was to avoid Manhattans. Because they're delicious.

A QUICK LAME LESSON ABOUT SCOTCH

SCOTCH is whiskey, and there are basically two kinds of whiskey. (There are also two spellings of whiskey: *whiskey* in the United States and Ireland, and *whisky* in Scotland, England, and Canada. And only the kind that is distilled in Scotland can be called scotch, just like sparkling wine can only legally be called Champagne if it is made in the Champagne region of France.)

THE first is single malt, which comes from a single distiller. There are distilleries all over Scotland (and the world), and each distillery makes a variety with a taste unique to it and to the land around it. In each brand, you can taste the earth and vegetation and climate and everything else unique to where that distillery is located. In the Islay region of Scotland, for example, you can taste the peat moss that's inherent in the ground. This makes Islay whiskies taste like you're drinking a log. That sounds terrible, but it's actually delicious, since it makes for a very smoky glass of booze. Some regions make for thinner whiskies. Others taste more like caramel. Whiskies from other countries have their own unique taste, too. Grab a few books and do a deep whiskey dive. It's worth your time. But for now, just know that single malts shouldn't really be used in mixed drinks unless they're specifically called for, because it's a

waste of their unique tastes. If you're making mixed drinks that are whiskey based, you should use the other type of whiskey . . .

. . . *Blended whiskey*. Why? Well, for consistency of taste. They've been formulated out of many different single malts in order to create a similar taste from bottle to bottle and batch to batch and, quite frankly, brand to brand. Blended whiskey brands include Johnnie Walker, Dewar's, and the Famous Grouse, to name but a few, and while they each have a signature taste, they're more consistent in flavor than single malts, thus ensuring that your whiskey cocktail recipes don't produce drinks that are wildly different. Blended whiskies are also usually less costly than single malts, although you can find higher quality and hence more expensive blended scotch, like Johnnie Walker Blue Label. But in general, a bottle of blended whiskey won't cost you an arm and a leg, and so you won't mind mixing it with other liquors.

OKAY, lesson over. Now, let's make a Manhattan!

Ice

2 ounces blended whiskey

1 ounce sweet vermouth

2 dashes of Angostura bitters (if you can find cherry bitters, use them instead)

Cocktail cherry (Luxardo, if you have it)

FILL a mixing glass with ice and add the whiskey, sweet vermouth, and bitters. Stir until cold and strain into a chilled cocktail glass. Drop in the cherry, and down the hatch! Your little town blues will go melting away!

VARIATIONS

FOR some people, a standard Manhattan is a bit on the sweet side. For them, try a Dry Manhattan by swapping in dry vermouth for the sweet vermouth.

OR you can try my personal favorite, a Perfect Manhattan, which uses a combo of dry and sweet vermouth. Just use ½ ounce of dry vermouth and ½ ounce of sweet vermouth and add them to the whiskey and bitters. Just like the name says . . . perfect!

COCKTAIL #6—DUBONNET COCKTAIL

THE QUEEN'S FAVORITE

The song—"LDN" by Lily Allen

For Laurie's fiftieth birthday, we met a few friends in the South of France to do a weeklong barge cruise down the Canal du Midi, which we'd done several times in the past and always had beautiful weather and an amazing experience. We even had the barge owners bring back a great London chef, Louie, from a previous trip and headed off down the canal for six days of sun and fun. We looked forward to Louie setting off every morning on his unicycle to gather whatever was fresh at the market and preparing delicious meals while we sat on the top deck sipping rosé and eating Lucques olives.

Thus went the wonderful first day, and we settled in for a heavenly trip.

Well, the next day it poured with rain. As it did the next day. And the next day. And the next day. It poured every second for the rest of our trip. And so we found ourselves all day, every day, sitting below deck on small sofas, reading books and drinking. One of our friends, pastry chef extraordinaire Eric Lanlard, had brought along a biography of the Queen Mother, and we took turns reading it to fill the time. The thing that stuck with us most from the book was that both the Queen Mother and Queen Elizabeth herself enjoyed a gin and Dubonnet every day of their adult lives. So of course we had to do the exact same thing.

What is Dubonnet? Well, technically, it's a sweet apéritif that's a blend of fortified wine, herbs, and spices, as well as a small amount of quinine. At least that's the technical definition. For our purposes here, it's a delicious mixer that is somewhere between a tawny port and a sweet vermouth. It comes in red, white, and gold varieties, but the red (Dubonnet Rouge) is the most popular. I'd start with that, and if you love it, you can try out the other two.

Since Dubonnet has so many different uses, and since there's no one definitive recipe to use it in, I've included three that I think are really good—plus a bonus royal recipe!

DUBONNET COCKTAIL

Ice
1½ ounces Dubonnet Rouge apéritif
1½ ounces gin

Dash of Angostura bitters
Lemon or orange twist

FILL a mixing glass with ice, then add the Dubonnet, gin, and bitters. Stir until cold. Strain into a chilled cocktail glass and garnish with a twist. Dubonn-yay!

DUBONNET HIGHBALL

Ice cubes
2 ounces Dubonnet Rouge apéritif

Club soda
Lemon twist

PLACE the ice cubes in a highball or Tom Collins glass and pour the Dubonnet over the ice. Top with club soda and stir. Garnish with a lemon twist. Hello, highball!

CORONATION COCKTAIL

Ice
¾ ounce gin

¾ ounce Dubonnet Rouge apéritif
¾ ounce dry vermouth

FILL a mixing glass with ice and pour in the gin, Dubonnet, and dry vermouth. Stir until cold. Strain into a chilled cocktail glass. Take a drink and feel like royalty!

THE QUEEN'S GIN AND DUBONNET

As an added bonus, here's how Queen Elizabeth has her daily gin and Dubonnet!

2 ice cubes
2 ounces Dubonnet Rouge apéritif

1 ounce gin
Lemon slice

PLACE 2 ice cubes in an old fashioned glass and add the Dubonnet and gin. Stir to combine and add the lemon. Drink before lunch if you want to be like the Queen. God save this drink!

COCKTAIL #7—BIJOU COCKTAIL

A DRINK WITH GREEN STUFF IN IT

The song—"Ghostbusters" by Ray Parker Jr.

Ice

¾ ounce gin

¾ ounce sweet
vermouth

¾ ounce green
Chartreuse herbal
liqueur

Dash of orange
bitters

Cocktail cherry

Yes, I made a reboot of the movie *Ghostbusters*. Some people liked it. Some people didn't like it. Some people got really angry about it. But I had a lot of fun making it and I'm proud of it and it won Favorite Movie at the Nickelodeon Kids' Choice Awards in 2017, so that was pretty cool. But some guys are still angry about it. I can't help that, but I *can* suggest they make one of these drinks and try to relax and remember it's just a movie.

In honor of *Ghostbusters* and ectoplasmic slime, I wanted to make a drink that had something green in it. Laurie and I discovered green Chartreuse several years ago while on a vacation in France and were so taken with it that we ordered an enormous bottle of it for our home bar. That bottle then sat in its box for years, untouched, because we didn't really know what to do with it, and then we forgot about it until I recently discovered it when I cleaned out the shelves under my bar.

Green Chartreuse is a tricky ingredient because (a) it's really high in alcohol, (b) it tastes a bit medicinal, and (c) it can easily overpower any drink. It's made with about 130 herbs, so there's a lot going on flavor-wise in that very innocent-looking light green liquid. There's definitely a licorice taste at the forefront, but it also has an absinthe quality to it. Just to get a handle on it, it's worth pouring yourself a small shot to get to know its upsides and downsides, because the very first time you encounter it in a mixed drink is always a bit of a shock.

I will say that green Chartreuse will really warm you up on a cold day. It's got a lovely afterburn as it heads down your throat looking for trouble. I would always bank on green Chartreuse winning whatever contest it enters. It's just that powerful!

The drink that seemed the best to introduce you to how green Chartreuse plays with others goes by three different names, according to the *Mr. Boston: Official Bartender's Guide*. It shows up as the Bijou Cocktail, the Jewel Cocktail, and the Tailspin Cocktail. Since my motivation to make this drink in the first place was *Ghostbusters*, we'll go with the Bijou, because that's what a lot of movie theaters used to be called. Bust it up!

FILL a mixing glass with ice, add the gin, sweet vermouth, Chartreuse, and bitters, and stir. Strain into a chilled cocktail glass. Add a cherry and sip like a Ghostbuster. I ain't 'fraid of this drink!

COCKTAIL #8—THE HOT TODDY!

The song—"Hot Hot Hot" by Buster Poindexter

1 sugar cube or
1 teaspoon honey

Boiling water

2 ounces blended
whiskey (definitely
not good single
malt)

Lemon slice

Whole nutmeg
seed

Hot booze? Hot damn!!! Hot alcoholic drinks have an old-timey feel to them, like in *It's a Wonderful Life* when Clarence the angel says something like, "I'll have a flaming rum punch, and be quick about it, me lad."

A toddy is pretty much just hot water with booze and something sweet in it. It's perfect for cold winter evenings and whenever you have a sore, scratchy, or simply tired throat. Serve it in a clear glass mug, if you can, so you can see its beautiful color and the lovely way it steams up the top of the glass. Hotty toddy!

HOT WHISKEY TODDY

PLACE the sugar cube or honey in a mug, then fill the mug two-thirds full of boiling water. Stir to dissolve the sugar or honey, then add the whiskey. Stir again and decorate with the lemon slice. Grate fresh nutmeg over the drink. Sip carefully so you don't burn yourself. Feel the heat!

HOT GIN TODDY

DO everything the same as above but substitute gin for the whiskey. That's it. Simple!

COCKTAIL #9—CLARIDGE COCKTAIL

The song—"Dancing with Myself" by Billy Idol

Ice

1½ ounces gin

1½ ounces dry vermouth

½ ounce Cointreau orange liqueur

½ ounce apricot brandy

Lemon twist

Claridge's Hotel in London is my favorite hotel in the world. Its elegant old-world charm is right in my sweet spot, since I'm British on my mother's side and love traditional English style. Laurie and I love getting cocktails and snacks in their beautiful little Fumoir Bar, which used to be dedicated to smokers, with its very high ceilings and dark walls that wouldn't show the smoke stains. You can't smoke in it anymore, but it's a wonderful place to spend an evening. So this cocktail first caught my eye in the *Mr. Boston* book because I figured it originated in the Fumoir. But then I found out that the drink is actually from the book *Barflies and Cocktails*, which was written by the staff of Harry's New York Bar in 1927. In that book, they say the cocktail is named after the Claridge Hotel in Paris, where it was invented by the head bartender. So, turns out it has nothing to do with Claridge's in London.

However, by the time I knew all of this I had already made the drink and liked it. So, origins aside, give it a whirl! But make sure you use apricot brandy. When I first made this, I used pear brandy instead and, well, it didn't quite work. With the apricot brandy, it is a drink worthy of whatever hotel you want to think it's named after. Okay, here we go!

FILL a cocktail shaker with ice, then add the gin, vermouth, Cointreau, and brandy. Shake, then strain into a chilled cocktail glass. Squeeze the lemon twist over the surface and drop it into the drink. Have a few of these and check into any hotel you want!

COCKTAIL #10—THE FEIGTINI

A PAUL FEIG ORIGINAL

The song—"One Step Beyond" by Madness

Ice

3 ounces gin

1 ounce sake

1 ounce Cointreau orange liqueur

Dash of orange bitters

Orange twist

Before we get to this quite delicious original drink I *invented* (Feig buffs nails on shirt), let's talk cocktail parties again.

When I was telling you how to throw the perfect cocktail party, I left out one small piece of advice. My good friend Tania Idle has a tradition she's been doing for years at her parties: She always keeps a small silver box filled with fake mustaches on her coffee table. Whenever the energy at her parties starts to flag, or if she just wants to kick things into high gear, she makes everybody put on a fake mustache.

It sounds crazy, but I've never seen it fail to work. People simply love wearing fake mustaches. It's funny and weirdly stylish, and you discover that some people look way better with a bit of facial hair, even if it's fake. Suddenly everybody is having the greatest time ever. Order a few packs of fake mustaches online and give it a try!

And now for the drink. When I first started doing my cocktail show to raise money for charity and cheer people up during the Covid-19 quarantine, I noticed the word *quarantini* was beginning to gain in popularity, but it didn't have an actual drink associated with it. Enterprising man that I am, I decided to invent one. And this is it! But, since the worst of the pandemic is now behind us, I figured the last thing any of us want to hear is the word *quarantine*. So I am proud to present to you . . . the Feigtini!

FILL a cocktail shaker with ice, then add the gin, sake, Cointreau, and bitters. Shake vigorously, then strain into a chilled cocktail glass. Garnish with the orange twist and Feig it up!

COCKTAIL #11—THE MODERN COCKTAIL

The song—"Burning Love" by Elvis Presley

¼ ounce fresh lemon juice

1 teaspoon honey

1 ounce peaty single-malt scotch whiskey (like Laphroaig or Ardbeg)

1 ounce sloe gin

Dash of absinthe

Dash of orange bitters

Ice

Cocktail cherry

A picture is worth a thousand words, as the old saying goes, and this picture says it all. Laurie, the Tipsy Faunt to my Drunk Funcle on my cocktail show, really hated this drink. And I'm not going to pretend it's not a challenging one. There's a lot going on in here. You've got smoke butting up against sweet, mixed in with bitter, coexisting with citrus, and then a cherry is thrown into the middle of it all for good measure.

This is what I love about cocktails and mixology, though. Anything can become a good drink, because everybody has different tastes. One person's terrible cocktail is another person's favorite. For many of us, a lot of cocktails simply fall in the middle. Some can be extremely challenging upon first taste, but as you keep sipping it, you start to discover things to like. Often it's about your expectations.

I find the same thing happens with movies. If you go into a movie expecting it to be one thing and it's not what you expected, your first instinct is that you didn't like it. But then when you run across it again on TV and know what to expect, you start to appreciate it for what it is.

So that's why I ask, isn't it better to try new things and see what you like and don't like? With that massive introduction and disclaimer, I now give you Tipsy's favorite . . . the Modern Cocktail!

STIR the lemon juice and honey in a cocktail shaker until dissolved. Add the whiskey, sloe gin, and the dashes, then add ice. Shake and strain into a chilled cocktail glass. Add the cherry and see what you think. How modern of you!

COCKTAIL #12—
HOT BUTTERED RUM

The song—"Southside Shuffle" by the J. Geils Band

1 tablespoon
butter

1 teaspoon brown
sugar or honey

Dash of ground
cinnamon

Dash of ground
nutmeg

Dash of ground
allspice

Splash of pure
vanilla extract

2 ounces dark rum

5 ounces hot
water

Cinnamon stick

I'd always heard of hot buttered rum but never really knew if it was real. It sounds like something from a Charles Dickens novel or something really extreme, as if you're shotgunning from the contraption that pours hot butter onto movie popcorn.

However, I eventually learned it's an actual drink and—surprise, surprise—it's really good! Don't believe me? Well, how dare you! I'm throwing down the gauntlet. I challenge you to make yourself one on a cold winter night. Or a hot summer night. Why the heck not? My mom always used to say that the best way to cool down on a hot day was to drink piping hot coffee. I'm guessing it's probably because you get so hot drinking it that, once you stop, everything else feels cooler. I'll leave it to scientists to say if that's actually true or if my mom was out of her mind.

Give this drink a whirl, simply because it's good and I think it'll make you happy. It's a real dickens of a drink! (I'm sorry.)

IN a coffee cup or Irish coffee mug, muddle the butter, brown sugar or honey, cinnamon, nutmeg, allspice, and vanilla until combined. (*Muddling* means smashing it all up in the bottom of the glass with a muddler or the handle of a wooden spoon.) Pour in the rum, then the hot water. Stir to mix thoroughly. Add a cinnamon stick and warm the cockles of your heart!

COCKTAIL #13—GIN SOUR

The song—"Can't Get You Out of My Head" by Kylie Minogue

Ice

1½ ounces gin

½ ounce Aperol aperitivo

1 ounce fresh lemon juice

1 egg white

Lemon wheel

Dash of Angostura bitters

Sours are great. Pure and simple. You can make sours out of just about any spirit. The "sour" part comes from adding lemon juice and some sort of sweetener, whether it's simple syrup or a sweet liqueur. The whiskey sour is probably the most famous sour out there, and we'll make that later on in the book (page 136). Right now, though, let's have a gin sour.

Some sours are made with raw egg whites and others aren't. Truth be told, you can usually do it either way; I know "raw egg white" doesn't seem like the most logical ingredient in a cocktail. And yes, there is a health risk, however slim, when you consume any part of a raw egg. But if you've got good fresh eggs, then odds are you're going to be fine, especially since the egg white is going into alcohol. If you have a health concern, skip the egg white, but it does add a delicious frothiness to the finished cocktail. Or you could use a vegan substitute (see page 137).

Ready to take a chance on something great? Then here's what you do . . .

FILL a cocktail shaker with ice and add the gin, Aperol, lemon juice, and egg white. Shake vigorously for 1 minute. Strain the drink into a separate shaker to get rid of the ice, then shake for another minute with no ice. Strain the drink into a chilled coupe or cocktail glass. Garnish with the lemon wheel, then sprinkle the bitters on top of the foam to decorate. Take a sip and see what you could have missed out on. Feel good about yourself for being so brave about booze!

A gin sour, complete with egg white. Go ahead, take a chance!

COCKTAIL #14—WOODWARD COCKTAIL

The song—"Think" by Aretha Franklin

Ice

1½ ounces blended scotch whiskey

½ ounce dry vermouth

1 tablespoon fresh grapefruit juice

I'm a proud Michigander. I grew up twenty minutes outside of Detroit. And in Detroit there is a main street called Woodward Boulevard that runs straight through the city. When I first saw this cocktail in the *Mr. Boston* book, I was drawn to it simply because of its name. But then I saw that it was a whiskey-based drink, and I had second thoughts about making it, because I like to share cocktails with my wife, and Tipsy Faunt isn't a big whiskey fan. It sounded good to me, though, and I decided to take a chance because of the grapefruit element. Tipsy loves grapefruit juice, and I was curious how much it would counteract the strong flavor of the scotch.

Well, she took a sip and declared that she liked it. So it passed the Tipsy test, and now I can pass it along to you with a clean conscience. Please enjoy my favorite Detroit-themed cocktail! Lions and Tigers and Wings, oh my!

FILL a cocktail shaker with ice, add the rest of the ingredients, and shake. Strain into a chilled cocktail glass and enjoy a taste of Motor City!

COCKTAIL #15—THE INCOME TAX COCKTAIL

The song—"She Works Hard for the Money" by Donna Summer

Ice

1½ ounces gin

¾ ounce dry vermouth

¾ ounce sweet vermouth

Juice of ¼ orange (about ½ ounce)

2 dashes of Angostura bitters

Orange wheel

Taxes. Nobody seems to like them. I don't get too upset about taxes because for me they're sort of the price of admission for living in a nice country. Still, they can be a bit annoying, especially when it comes to having to actually *do* your taxes each April. But like all good citizens, we do the right thing and get them done. It's not fun, though.

How do you make it more fun? Well, you have a cocktail named after it all. Enter the Income Tax cocktail. Despite its unpleasant name, I'll just say that this cocktail will make you very happy. It's a crowd-pleaser because all of its ingredients are hard to dislike. Both the dry and sweet varieties of vermouth go down very easy, and who doesn't enjoy orange juice? And as we discussed earlier, the great thing about gin is that you can always find one that suits your palate. My own brand, Artingstall's, works very nicely in this cocktail because it doesn't jump too far forward in the juniper/pine taste area. Its citrus qualities work nicely with both the juice and the vermouths. But you can also make this drink much more gin-forward if you want to go with a stronger gin, like a Beefeater or Berry Bros. & Rudd "#3." Or you can just find one you like somewhere in the middle.

The bottom line is this is a nice, complex-tasting, yet easy-to-make drink. Give it a whirl and you'll see what I mean. And that won't be taxing at all! (I'm sorry, again.)

FILL a cocktail shaker with ice, add the gin, dry and sweet vermouths, orange juice, and bitters, and shake. Strain into a chilled cocktail glass. Garnish with an orange wheel and use the cocktail as an excuse to put off doing your taxes until tomorrow!

COCKTAIL #16—CELEBRATION COCKTAIL

The song—"C'est la Vie" by Khaled

Ice

1 ounce Cognac

1 ounce red sweet vermouth

1 ounce Italian bitter aperitivo, such as Campari

2 dashes of orange bitters

Orange twist

Tipsy and I are big fans of celebrating. We celebrate successes, failures, good days, bad days—pretty much everything. Why? Because we're alive and we have great friends and because we should always be grateful for getting through another day. Cocktails are part of that celebration for us. So I searched the internet to see if there was a drink called the Celebration Cocktail and, lo and behold, I found a recipe on several sites.

If you look closely at this cocktail and have been reading this book in order, you may realize that there's something familiar about this recipe. Want to take a guess? I'll give you a minute.

Okay, minute's up. This drink is basically a Negroni, but instead of gin it uses Cognac. The three main ingredients are all used in equal amounts, just like in a Negroni, but it adds some orange bitters and subtracts the ice in the cocktail glass. It also has an orange twist like a Negroni. But it tastes a lot different.

Shake one of these babies up and celebrate whatever you want to. Your life, your family, the Earth, your pets. Whatever. Just celebrate!

FILL a mixing glass with ice and add the Cognac, vermouth, bitter aperitivo, and orange bitters. Stir until very cold. Strain into a chilled coupe or cocktail glass. Garnish with an orange twist. Hooray! It's a celebration!

COCKTAIL #17—VIEUX CARRÉ

The song—"Les Cactus" by Jacques Dutronc

Ice

1 ounce rye whiskey

1 ounce Cognac

1 ounce sweet vermouth

½ teaspoon Bénédictine herbal liqueur

2 dashes of Angostura bitters

2 dashes of Peychaud's bitters

Lemon twist

Ooo la la! This French-sounding drink is actually inspired by the French Quarter in New Orleans. It contains some pretty heavy-duty ingredients and reads a bit like a classy Long Island Iced Tea. While it's not as nuts as that drink, it definitely packs a punch.

It also contains one of the trickier ingredients in the world of cocktails: Bénédictine. Made in France, with reportedly only three people in the world knowing the recipe at any one time, Bénédictine is a very herby liqueur that has a sweet, honeylike aftertaste. Used too liberally in a cocktail, it can overtake the subtler flavors other ingredients may bring to the drink.

But Bénédictine is used to great and restrained effect in the Vieux Carré. It helps that both Cognac and rye whiskey are not timid ingredients and can stand up to Bénédictine's bullying. The addition of two types of bitters also helps to tamp down Bénédictine's ego. What you're left with is a slightly caramelly drink that seems a lot more innocent than it actually is. It's really quite delightful. But don't take my word for it. See for yourself!

FILL a cocktail shaker with ice, add the rye, Cognac, vermouth, Bénédictine, and bitters, and shake. Strain into a highball glass over fresh ice. Garnish with a lemon twist. *Laissez les bons temps rouler!* Hoo-eee!

COCKTAIL #18—SINGAPORE SLING

The song—"Get the Party Started" by P!nk

Ice

1 ounce gin

1 ounce kirschwasser (cherry brandy)

1 ounce Bénédictine herbal liqueur

Club soda

Long lime peel

When I was doing an international press tour to promote *Ghostbusters: Answer the Call*, our first stop was in Singapore. I had never been before and it was wonderful. It was hot as a sauna because we were there in July, but wonderful nonetheless. As a cocktail fanatic, the one place I knew I had to go was Raffles Hotel, where they are famous for their Singapore Sling.

Tipsy, Melissa McCarthy, some members of our PR teams, and I went there and ordered the famous drink. A lovely blend of fruit and booze, it didn't disappoint. The first one went down very smooth. As did the second one. And, I believe, the third one. A Singapore Sling is one of those slightly evil drinks that doesn't really taste like a cocktail. The sweetness and density of the juices involved mask the alcoholic nature of the drink.

Which is why I really like this recipe. The Raffles version has a good amount of pineapple juice, as well as lime juice and triple sec, which tilts it in the sweet nectar direction. My version shifts the emphasis to the booze, the reason you're drinking a cocktail in the first place.

So give this version a whirl and enjoy its vacationy, boozy charms!

FILL a mixing glass or cocktail shaker with ice and add the gin, brandy, and Bénédictine, and shake. Strain into a Collins glass. Top with club soda, garnish with a long lime peel, and sling it back, baby!

COCKTAIL #19—MOJITO

The song—"Havana" by Camila Cabello

3 fresh mint leaves, plus more for garnish

2 ounces white rum

¾ ounce fresh lime juice (if using the standard method) or 1 lime (if using Alessandro's method)

½ ounce simple syrup (page 112)

Ice

Club soda

Lime wheel

Everybody loves mojitos. It's true. Ask anybody and their eyes will light up as they say, "I *love* mojitos!" Why? Because what's not to love?! They've got rum in them, which most people like. But even if they don't (like Tipsy), mojitos have mint, lime juice, and sugar to cover the rum up and transform the whole drink into a delicious adult punch.

Now, this recipe is one in which you muddle mint in the shaker before you add the other ingredients, then once it's all mixed up you strain it into the glass, leaving the spent mint in the shaker. But my good friend, mixologist extraordinaire Alessandro Palazzi, muddles not only the mint but also lime wedges in the serving glass to extract the juice, and he then leaves them in to mix with the rest of the ingredients and serves it all as one. I have to say, it's a very pretty presentation and makes the drink even more festive than it already is. You'll just need to use a bigger glass to hold it all.

If you try Alessandro's method, make sure you use a sturdy glass, and don't use a metal muddler because it will most likely break the glass. Use a wooden muddler, which is really the best kind anyway, or our old friend the wooden mixing spoon handle.

Okay, ready for a sipping trip to Cuba? Here's your passport!

STANDARD METHOD: Muddle the mint lightly in a shaker, then add the rum, lime juice, and simple syrup. Add ice and shake briefly, then strain into a Tom Collins or highball glass with fresh ice. Top with club soda and garnish with a mint sprig and the lime wheel. Go go, mojito!

ALESSANDRO'S METHOD: Cut a whole lime into 4 wedges, then cut each wedge in half. Place the pieces in a large water glass (since this version of the drink takes up more room than your standard highball glass) along with the mint and muddle thoroughly to get all the juice out of the limes. Add the rum and simple syrup, then put in a lot of ice and stir. Top with club soda and garnish with a mint sprig and the lime wheel. *Salud, porque belleza sobra,* as they say in Cuba, meaning "To your health, since you're already so beautiful!" Indeed!

COCKTAIL #20—SWEET MARTINI

The song—"Just One Dance" by Caro Emerald

Ice

1 ounce gin

1 ounce sweet vermouth

Dash of orange bitters

Dash of orange Curaçao

Lemon twist

Let's talk about sweet drinks. Some people love them. Others hate them. Cocktail purists tend to look down on them, or at least they look down on sugary drinks like the Lemon Drop and Sex on the Beach. But those cocktails tend to involve sugary ingredients like cranberry juice and simple syrup and sweet, fruity liqueurs like Midori and peach schnapps.

However, there are also "sweet drinks" that get to keep their cool titles. They tend to be the ones that involve sweet but aficionado-respected ingredients like sweet vermouth and Curaçao. It's all a bit snobby, but you're less likely to get side eye from a bartender in a classy joint if you order a Manhattan than you would if you asked for a Blue Hawaiian.

Should you even care what the bartender thinks of you? Hell no. If you want a Long Island Iced Tea or a Mai Tai with an umbrella sticking out of it, you should order it proudly. Nobody should ever tell you your tastes are wrong. You like what you like, and you should always feel free to let your freak flag fly!

That said, here's a nice recipe for something called a Sweet Martini. It's really good and is filled with classy ingredients, so if the bartender gives you a funny look when you order it, you can give them a funny look right back and say, "Do you not know what's in the drink?" and then explain it to them. That'll show 'em!

And now . . .

FILL a cocktail shaker with ice, add the gin, vermouth, bitters, and Curaçao, shake, and strain into a chilled cocktail glass. Squeeze the lemon twist over the surface of the martini and rub it around the lip of the glass. Drop the twist into the drink. How sweet it is!

COCKTAIL #21—CAMPARI COSMO

ANOTHER PAUL FEIG ORIGINAL

The song—"September" by Earth, Wind & Fire

I invented this drink on my cocktail show when I wanted to make a Cosmo but didn't have any cranberry juice and wasn't able to go pick any up because we were in the early days of quarantine and I was too scared to leave my house. But I realized that the cranberry juice in a Cosmo is really there more as a coloring agent than an actual taste ingredient; you use a dash or two to give it its pink color.

So, enterprising young man that I am, I looked for something else in my bar that was the color of cranberry juice and found my bottle of Campari. And then I realized that putting a bit of a bitter taste into a drink that is on the sweeter side might not be a bad thing. And it wasn't!

So here it is, my very own take on the infamous Cosmopolitan, something I like to call a Campari Cosmo. Campari and compare!

FILL a cocktail shaker with ice, add the vodka, Cointreau, lime juice, and Campari, shake, and strain into a chilled cocktail glass. Garnish with a lime wheel or slice. How cosmopolitan of you!

COCKTAIL #22—THE BEE'S KNEES

The song—"My House" by Flo Rida

This drink requires a bit of preparation, which opens up a question for any aspiring mixologist: How much work do you actually want to do? I fall in the category of the lazy bartender. I love making drinks from ingredients that are already in the bottles on my bar. I don't even make my own simple syrup, even though it's super-easy to do. I'm just not that finicky of a drinker.

There are some amazing books on the market, like *Liquid Intelligence* by Dave Arnold, that are all about making your own ingredients for cocktails. Some of them sound delicious and super-adventurous. One of my good friends is Boston bartender Todd Maul, who is like a mad scientist. He uses centrifuges and liquid nitrogen and reduces old Champagne into pastes that he then paints into the bottoms of cocktail glasses, and he even has a machine that crushes sugarcane to extract its syrup. His drinks are masterpieces.

But that's way too much work for me.

The great thing about mixology is you can be as ambitious or as lazy as you want, and you're going to get great drinks either way. It's much more impressive to hand somebody a drink and then tell them about the hours of work and scientific methodology that went into the making of them, but it's just as impressive to hand somebody a perfectly made martini or Negroni that uses regular store-bought ingredients and see their faces light up when they taste it.

Make your bartending skills match your passions in life. If you love complexity, dive into scientific mixology. If you love simplicity, master the basics. I've always found there are two types of people in life: Type 1, who walks into a house for sale and, no matter how nice it is, wants to tear it up and change everything; and Type 2, who looks for the perfect house so they can just move in and set up their stuff. I'm

Ice

2 ounces gin

¾ ounce fresh
lemon juice

½ ounce honey
syrup (recipe
below)

definitely a Type 2 but have a lot of Type 1 friends. And there's nothing wrong with being either type.

This was all a long windup to prepare you for the fact that this drink requires preparing one of the ingredients on the stove. Get to work! (Or move on to the next drink, you lazy bastard.)

FILL a cocktail shaker with ice, add the gin, lemon juice, and honey syrup, shake, and strain into a chilled cocktail glass. One taste and you'll see it truly is the bee's knees!

HONEY SYRUP

IN a small saucepan, place ½ cup honey and ½ cup water and set over medium heat. Stir until just blended (don't boil or reduce it) and pour into a sterilized jar or squeeze bottle. Any extra you have after making the drink will last up to 1 month in the refrigerator.

COCKTAIL #23—AMERICANO

The song—"Americano" by the Brian Setzer Orchestra

Ice

1½ ounces Campari aperitivo

1½ ounces sweet vermouth

Club soda

Orange twist

Not all cocktails have to pack a punch. Some of them, like spritzes, are simply there to usher you into your evening like a friendly Boy Scout helping you across the street. They are made with a lower percentage of alcohol and are cut with soda water, so they don't make you feel like you're having "a drink." They're almost like taking a break. "We've been out walking around all day. Should we stop and have a little something?" That's the attitude I usually find results in my hand wrapped around a glass containing some sort of nice, cold, bubbly aperitivo with a bit of fruit in it when Laurie and I find ourselves on vacation somewhere in Italy. And it always makes me happy.

An Americano is basically a spritz. It's two mixers that usually play second fiddle to the first-chair spirit who have now been given their own orchestra and told to put on a concert. The lovely clash between the sweet and bitter is softened by the club soda and allowed to dance on your tongue before quenching your thirst.

I guess that's also the lovely thing about spritzes—it's okay to face them as a thirst-quenching beverage instead of as a cocktail. You don't reach for a martini because you're feeling dry and parched. You drink it because you want to savor it. While you'll also savor a spritz, it's the adult equivalent of drinking your favorite soda on a hot day—it tastes great and it quenches your thirst.

While I don't advocate chugging an Americano like you're in a Gatorade commercial, I do suggest you mix up one of these on a hot summer day and sip your way to refreshment!

PLACE ice in a Tom Collins or highball glass and add the Campari and vermouth. Add soda to fill and garnish with an orange twist. *Salute!*

COCKTAIL #24—TOM COLLINS, FEIG-STYLE

The song—"You Got to Have a Mother for Me" by James Brown

Ice

2 ounces gin

1 ounce fresh lemon juice

1 ounce simple syrup (page 112)

Cocktail cherry

Orange slice

Okay, what started as a mistake when I first made this drink on my cocktail show has turned into a recipe variation I'm proud to put my name on. All Tom Collins recipes call for club soda, but I was doing a live show from my guesthouse and had forgotten my bottle of soda water in the kitchen. (Oh sure, some lesser entertainer would have left the audience hanging as they went off to fix the mistake, but I'm simply too much of a professional!) So, I put in more ice cubes than you normally would and filled my Tom Collins glass with all the ingredients except for the soda.

The result? An absolutely delicious drink that is pretty much the boozy equivalent of lemonade. Filling the glass with extra ice adds a bit of dilution, but less than if you added the club soda. The result is a stronger, sweeter drink that highlights all the tastes within it. Sure, it would be great with the club soda too, but both Tipsy and I really loved the intensity of this drink sans bubbles.

Whip one up and give it a try. You can compare it to the traditional way that appears on page 112. How you Tom is totally up to you!

FILL a cocktail shaker with ice, add the gin, lemon juice, and simple syrup, shake, and strain into a Tom Collins glass filled two-thirds with ice cubes. Garnish with a cherry and orange slice. What a delicious mistake!

A STANDARD TOM COLLINS

FOLLOW the recipe on page 110 but add 2 ounces of club soda to the glass after shaking the cocktail. Fill the glass only halfway with ice to make room for the club soda. Standard but stunning!

HOW TO MAKE YOUR OWN SIMPLE SYRUP

You can buy ready-made simple syrups at several price points. Some are higher end, made with cane sugar, and some are lower end, made with high-fructose corn syrup. I suggest either going for the higher end syrup or simply making your own. It's super-easy and you'll know you're using real sugar, as opposed to whatever the hell high-fructose corn syrup is.

Combine ½ cup granulated sugar and ½ cup water in a small saucepan over medium heat and stir occasionally until the sugar is dissolved. Once cool, store in a sterilized jar with a lid in the refrigerator. It will last up to 1 month.

COCKTAIL #25—
EL PRESIDENTE

The song—"You Should Be Dancing" by the Bee Gees

I tried to be a president once. It was in the sixth grade, and I ran for president of my class. I promised everything under the sun to my classmates (free pizza, weekly parties, and help with homework, just to name but a few of my campaign vows) because I wanted to win that title more than anything in the world. And I ended up winning! I was beside myself with joy. I, the bullied and nerdy Paul Feig, was the actual president of my peers.

Sadly, my enthusiasm for winning only lasted up to the Election Day returns, and once I had the title, I completely lost interest in the actual job of presidenting.

My classmates would ask me where the free pizza was, when the parties were happening, and how quickly I could complete their homework for them. I blew them all off presidentially and went about my normal life. When the grumbling soon began, my teacher noticed, and as it intensified with each passing day, she decided that (a) I was a terrible president, and (b) this was an opportunity for a learning experience. One day she said to the class, "How are we all feeling about Paul as president?" to which everyone booed and catcalled. I was shocked for some reason (the hubris of youth or just the delusions of a slightly spoiled only child?) and looked around at the angry faces of my fellow students. It was then that my teacher uttered the words I'll

never forget—"Well, then this is a good way for us all to learn about the concept in government of 'impeachment.'"

And so I was impeached as president of my sixth grade class.

This cocktail with a great name (despite its painful memories for a disgraced ineffective ex-leader) is a very pretty drink that benefits not only visually but taste-wise from the addition of a cocktail cherry. But remember what I advised earlier on page 33: Use a real cocktail cherry (like a Luxardo), the kind that are very dark and come in a dark syrup, not one of those nasty neon red maraschinos you find in ice cream parlors. Those nuclear ones won't give you the rich cherry flavor you need here, and they're also terrible for you. Not that drinking cocktails is the world's healthiest hobby, but if you're going to do it, try to use the best ingredients you can afford. It's what a true El Presidente would do!

Ice

1 ounce light rum

1 ounce dry vermouth

1 teaspoon grenadine

1 teaspoon orange Curaçao

Orange twist

Cocktail cherry

Cherry syrup (optional)

FILL a mixing glass with ice, then add the rum and vermouth. Stir until cold and add the grenadine and Curaçao. Stir again and strain into a chilled cocktail glass. Twist the orange peel over the surface to release the oil, then drop in the peel and the cherry. Add a little drip of the syrup that the cherries come in if you'd like a bit of extra cherry taste. Hail to the Chief!

COCKTAIL #26—IRISH COFFEE

The song—"Egg Man" by the Beastie Boys

Another hot drink! Woo-hoo!

Tipsy and I first went to Ireland for Christmas back in the 1990s and just loved it. The green of the scenery is so rich and deep that it immediately stirs something in you, whether you have any Irish in your DNA or not. But it was the first time we had real Irish coffee there that we truly shouted "*Erin go bragh!*" (Which means "Ireland till the end of time," in case you were wondering exactly what you were drunkenly yelling on St. Patrick's Day in your favorite Irish pub.)

Irish coffee may just be sweet, boozy coffee with whipped cream on top, but the key to making it great is to use great ingredients. Start with excellent java. Laurie and I order coffee beans from our favorite coffee place in Rome, the famous Sant'Eustachio il Caffè. The resulting brew has such a rich and powerful flavor that, when you use it in Irish coffee, you can really taste the difference more than if you were to use a light grocery-store brand. Wherever you get your coffee from, go for a stronger-tasting variety, regardless—La Colombe works great, and so does Starbucks.

The same goes with the whiskey; use an Irish whiskey that you can also enjoy on its own. You can never go wrong with Jameson or Bushmills. I was once given what I thought was a bottle of cheap Irish whiskey as a gift and used it to make Irish coffee, then discovered that it was actually a very expensive bottle. People gave me a hard time for "wasting" it, but I have to say, it made for one of the best Irish coffees I've ever had outside of Ireland.

The other key ingredient is the whipped cream. Don't use sweetened whipped cream, because there's sugar in the drink itself and you don't want it to taste like dessert. An Irish coffee may be great at the end of a meal, but it shouldn't taste like a hot milkshake. One of the best Irish coffees I've ever had was at the Gritti Palace in Venice, Italy. Instead of whipped cream, they use a whipped panna da montare. It's thicker than whipped cream, has less fat, and isn't sweet. But it has a frozen quality to it that makes it a comforting bit of ice cream–like goodness that then gives way to the hot, spiked coffee underneath. Absolute heaven. Try looking around online to see if you can find some recipes to make your own panna. It's worth it!

And now, without further ado, heeeeeere's . . . Irish coffee!!!

1½ ounces Irish whiskey

2 teaspoons packed dark brown sugar

Hot coffee (regular or decaf)

Unsweetened whipped cream (homemade if possible; see Note)

TO heat an Irish coffee mug or glass, fill it with hot water, then pour the water out once the glass is hot. Add the whiskey and brown sugar to the mug and stir until the sugar is dissolved, then add the coffee to fill, leaving room for the whipped cream. Top with the whipped cream, and down the hatch! (But don't burn yourself.) *Sláinte!*

NOTE: To make your own unsweetened whipped cream, simply put 1 cup of heavy cream into a bowl and, using a whisk (if you're in the mood for a good workout) or an electric mixer (if you're not), whip the cream until soft peaks form. Be careful not to overwhip it or it could get a rather grainy texture, which would just make your Irish coffee sad.

COCKTAIL #27—MARGARITAS!

The song—"Tijuana Taxi" by Herb Alpert & the Tijuana Brass

Oh, tequila. Why are you so many things to so many different people? I have a lot of friends who love tequila. I've had some of the finest sipping tequilas in fancy restaurants and enjoyed them like a great glass of single malt. And yet, for some reason, I always feel like tequila knocks me on my ass. One of the worst hangovers I've ever had in my life was after a night of doing tequila shots with beer chasers. I was absolutely green the next day. But in retrospect, I blame the shots more than I blame the tequila.

Let's take this moment to discuss the whole concept of "shots." To me, shots are not about enjoying alcohol. They're about getting drunk. Why else would you knock a drink back that fast? You don't chug a cocktail. You sip it and enjoy it. You expect it to taste good and judge the drink as you slowly consume it. You savor it.

Shots are like dares. "I dare you to drink all of this in one swig." People pour out shots when they want to get the party started. But I find that laying a baseline of shots as the foundation to your evening is like wolfing down a whole turkey before entering a hot dog–eating contest. If the drink doesn't taste good enough to sip, then why bother drinking it? If you're just looking to get drunk, why not at least put the booze on the rocks and sip as you loosen up with your friends? Why do you want to set your course to throw up halfway through the evening and feel awful the next day?

I say have more respect for both yourself and the tequila and enjoy it in something great. Like a margarita!

What is there to say about margaritas that hasn't been said? They're delicious, they're fun, they look great, and they make everybody happy. But I used to avoid margaritas, because the idea of drinking that sugary yellowish-green-looking margarita mix I would see in those plastic bottles they sell in stores felt like I'd be ordering the equivalent of a glass of Mountain Dew. But then I realized that real margaritas don't use mixes—they contain just three simple yet elegant ingredients that blend together perfectly.

My advice is to avoid those margarita mixes at all costs. No one needs that much sugar in a drink, especially when making a margarita with the real ingredients results in a much better beverage. So get out your lime squeezer and prepare yourself a delicious *real* margarita, one worthy of the great liquor that is tequila. If you want to put salt on the rim, that's delicious, too! Just don't use table salt. Your marg would never forgive you.

Lime wedge

Margarita salt or coarse kosher salt

Crushed ice

1½ ounces tequila

Juice of 1 large lime

½ ounce Cointreau orange liqueur or triple sec

TO prep the glass, rub the rim of a margarita glass or old fashioned glass with a lime wedge to wet it, then dip the rim in a plate of the salt. (Assuming you want a salt rim. If you don't, skip this step.)

FILL a cocktail shaker with ice, add the tequila, lime juice, and Cointreau, and shake. Pour the drink and ice into the glass without straining. *Salud!*

COCKTAIL #28—MILK PUNCH

The song—"Love Shack" by the B-52's

Crushed ice

Ice cubes

1 ounce brandy

½ ounce dark rum

2 teaspoons simple syrup (page 112)

2 dashes of pure vanilla extract

4 ounces whole milk (use lactose-free milk if you have issues with dairy)

Crushed ice

Whole nutmeg seed

Milk punch? Milk in an alcoholic drink? That sounds awful.

Or does it?

It turns out that dairy products and alcohol can actually be friends. Ever have a White Russian? Delish! Ever have a Brandy Alexander? Wowee! It turns out drinks that use milk or cream are insanely good. Whatever fears I had that the milk would curdle the minute it hit the booze evaporated the second I poured out and tasted my first milk punch. For me, this was the gateway drink to dessert cocktails involving heavy cream. (More about them coming up later.)

So don't be afraid. Look at these ingredients. They're fantastic. Even Tipsy liked this drink, and she doesn't really like rum or brandy. But the vanilla landed the plane for her. It's always milk punch ahoy in the Feig house now! Give it a whirl!

FILL a cocktail shaker with ice cubes and add the brandy, rum, simple syrup, vanilla, and milk. Shake and strain into tumbler filled with crushed ice. Grate fresh nutmeg on top, and down this dairy delight. Cow sweet it is! (At some point I'll have to stop apologizing for these puns.)

COCKTAIL #29—WAIKIKI BEACHCOMBER

The song—"Love Machine" by the Miracles

Ice

1 ounce gin

1 ounce Cointreau
orange liqueur or
triple sec

½ ounce pineapple
juice

What's more delicious than pineapple juice? Nothing! It's the juice that never fails to please. If we had to vote on an official nectar of the Gods, my vote would go to pineapple juice. It's great on its own but even better as a mixer. One of my favorite nonalcoholic beverages is a glass of half fresh pineapple juice and half club soda. A pineapple soda, if you will. It's mighty tasty and also way better for you than soda pop.

While this drink has a name evocative of a vacation in the tropics, you can drink it anytime, anywhere. It's a real crowd-pleaser that's as easy to make as it is to drink. There are only three ingredients, and each of them is great on its own: gin, Cointreau or triple sec, and pineapple juice. I always use Cointreau when given a choice between Cointreau and triple sec; I find it to be a more nuanced liqueur. Sometimes I'll also substitute Curaçao, since they're all orange-flavored. But any of them will work, and you'll discover your personal preferences the more you use these ingredients.

Now put on your lei, break out your ukulele, and mix yourself up a mini-vacation in a glass!

FILL a cocktail shaker with ice and add the gin, Cointreau or triple sec, and pineapple juice. Shake and strain into a chilled cocktail glass. HipaHipa!

COCKTAIL #30—CANADIAN CHERRY

The song—"Lady of the 80's" by Loverboy

1½ ounces
Canadian whisky

½ ounce
kirschwasser
(cherry brandy),
plus more to taste

¼ ounce fresh
lemon juice

¼ ounce fresh
orange juice

Ice

My mom was Canadian. I have dual Canadian and United States citizenship. I love Canada. I officiated the wedding of Bruce McCulloch of *Kids in the Hall* to his wife, Tracy, using my status as an ordained minister procured online through the Universal Life Church. A head of the ULC once kept me on the phone for an hour talking about how guys don't know how to check themselves for testicular cancer, but he wasn't Canadian, so I'm not sure why I told you that.

But the bottom line is I have Canada in my blood. I grew up in Detroit and my parents had a little cottage on Lake Erie outside of Windsor, Ontario, just over the river from Detroit. I was on the Canadian Bozo show when I was five. And my friend and I used to drive to Canada when I was nineteen to avoid Michigan's drinking age of twenty-one. So Canadian boozing and I go a long way back.

I remember when I was a kid my mom would drive us over to Windsor to take the train to Toronto, where she'd lived and worked as a telephone operator before I was born. It was her favorite city in the world, and we'd spend a few days walking around and going to all her most beloved places. But my most vivid memory is of getting on the train in Windsor. We'd always get there before the sun came up, and the train station was next to the Johnnie Walker plant. The smell of whatever malt they were putting in that whiskey was really strong and was quite a wake-up call that early in the morning. I can still conjure up that sense memory to this day.

This drink reminds me of all the above. The Canadian whisky plucks my Canadian heartstrings and the cherry brandy reminds me of Michigan, which is all about cherries. They even make cherry wine in my home state. So mix up one of these, turn on a hockey game, be extra polite, and enjoy, eh! (And yes, I just reduced Canada down to a cultural stereotype. My fellow Canadians might mind, but they're too nice to make me feel bad about it.)

SHAKE all the ingredients in a cocktail shaker with ice and strain into an old fashioned glass over fresh ice. Moisten the rim of the glass with a little extra cherry brandy to taste. It's a beauty way to go!

COCKTAIL #31—GIN CAESAR

The song—"Wings" by Little Mix

Lemon wedges

Celery salt

Ice

1 ounce gin

2 dashes of hot sauce

4 dashes of Worcestershire sauce

3 grinds of fresh salt and pepper

4 ounces Clamato juice, purchased or homemade (recipe follows)

Celery stalk

Lime wedge

Okay, we're not out of Canada yet.

If you've ever had brunch in Canada, you'll have noticed one big difference Americans have with our neighbors to the north. In the United States, we drink bloody Marys with our Sunday meal. But in Canada, they drink Caesars. What's the difference? Why, it's the magnificent mollusk known as the clam. Do they put clams in their drink? No, that would be awful. But they do use its juice in a little thing known as Clamato juice.

When I first heard of Clamato juice, I thought I was going to throw up. I like clams and always order spaghetti alle vongole when I'm in Italy. But for some reason the idea of clam juice permanently fused with tomato juice sounded as appetizing as worm-infused orange juice. But then a director friend of mine would always crack open a tallboy of Budweiser & Clamato Chelada at the end of a long day in the editing room, and it looked intriguing, so I tasted it. It was really good, and so I then changed my tune on Caesars.

I'm glad I did. They're a bit brinier than bloody Marys and tend to be a bit spicier. Clamato juice is a little lighter in texture than tomato juice, too, so these cocktails go down pretty quickly. One thing to know about Clamato juice, though, is that it's pretty high in sugar. So a Caesar isn't the healthiest drink you could make, but it's a fun Sunday treat.

If you want to make your own Clamato juice sans sugar, try the recipe on the next page. Homemade Clamato juice is pretty darn good.

The change I make to the traditional Caesar is to substitute gin for the vodka. I think it adds a bit more complexity. I do very much recommend my Artingstall's Brilliant London Dry Gin for this recipe, since a more juniper-forward gin might take over the drink more than you would like. Other gins you could use for this would be Hendrick's, Oxley, or Sacred. They're all on the mellower side.

Now, clam up and dive into a Gin Caesar! Take off!

RUB a lemon wedge on the rim of a Tom Collins glass to wet it, and then dip the rim in a plate of celery salt. Fill the glass to the top with ice. Add the gin, hot sauce, Worcestershire sauce, salt and pepper, and Clamato juice, in that order, and stir to mix. Add the celery stalk and lemon and lime wedges and sprinkle a little more celery salt on top if you want. Hail, Caesar!

HOMEMADE CLAMATO JUICE

Recipe courtesy of Serene Herrera at houseofyumm.com

2 cups tomato juice

½ cup clam juice

2 teaspoons Worcestershire sauce

1 teaspoon hot sauce

2 tablespoons fresh lemon juice

¼ teaspoon celery salt

½ teaspoon coarse black pepper

COMBINE all the ingredients in a medium bowl and whisk together. Store in a sealed container in the refrigerator for 5 to 7 days. Stir again before using.

COCKTAIL #32—THE GOLDEN DAWN

The song—"Saturday Night's Alright for Fighting" by Elton John

Ice

¾ ounce Calvados apple brandy

¾ ounce dry gin

¾ ounce Cointreau orange liqueur

¾ ounce apricot brandy

¾ ounce fresh orange juice

Cocktail cherry

Grenadine or cherry syrup

This is a great drink. There's a lot going on in it. It's an old drink, about which our good friend Dr. Cocktail says in his amazing book *Vintage Spirits and Forgotten Cocktails*, "It was judged 'World's Finest Cocktail' in the United Kingdom Bartenders' Guild contest in 1930." So I'm not kidding when I say it's good. It's so good that Tipsy loved it—and it includes several ingredients she doesn't like. I rest my case.

As a guy who has invented several drinks, I'm quite frankly jealous of this cocktail. I want to invent a cocktail that's called "World's Finest Cocktail" by a bunch of English bartenders. Or American bartenders. Or *any* bartenders. See, I'm a nice guy, but I'm extremely competitive. I'm not competitive at sports because I'm terrible at sports and don't even try to win when I get roped into some sort of sporting activity. I got talked into joining a softball team a few years ago because I was told it would be fun and "not serious" and ended up getting yelled at constantly by the ultracompetitive second baseman, who got mad at everything I did. So screw sports.

But I'm competitive at everything else. Like showbiz. And cocktail inventing. And gin making. One of the happiest days of my life was in 2019 when I found out Artingstall's won Best Gin and Double Gold at the Wine & Spirits Wholesalers of America tasting contest, the very first competition we'd entered. Because something I did won something.

Why did I tell you all this? Because I didn't know what else to write about the Golden Dawn other than it's really good and I wish I invented it. So make yourself this winner!

FILL a cocktail shaker with ice and add the Calvados, gin, Cointreau, brandy, and orange juice. Shake and strain into a chilled cocktail glass. Drop a cherry into the drink so that it sinks to the bottom, then drizzle in a little grenadine or cherry syrup from the jar. Do not stir. The grenadine or syrup should sit at the bottom with the cherry. Now you're golden!

COCKTAIL #33—HARVEY WALLBANGER

The song—"Disco Inferno" by the Trammps

Ice

1½ ounces vodka

4 ounces fresh orange juice

½ ounce Galliano herbal liqueur

Cocktail cherry

Orange slice

Oh man, was I into disco in my teens. I grew up in suburban Detroit in the 1970s and really embraced the disco fashions. Even though I did own a leisure suit at one point, I didn't dress like a cartoon of a guy who was into disco. True, I bought platform shoes once and my dad got mad at me because he wanted me to wear galoshes over them in the rain and none of them would fit over the clunky soles. I remember my dad down on his knees trying to force the rubber boots over the huge heel of one of the shoes, swearing a blue streak as he kept saying, "Oh, for God's sake, these stupid shoes!"

But by the time I started going to the teen disco that had opened in the bar of our local bowling alley, I was stylin'. It was all about Angel's Flight bell-bottom pants and wide-lapeled jackets and faux silk shirts with the collar out and my high-heeled pointy disco boots. I loved to dance and fancied myself quite the Gene Kelly of the dance floor. Of course, this was painfully disproven when I entered a disco dance contest one night and moved around the floor like James Brown's uncoordinated little brother. I thought I was killing it but then saw the impassive faces of all the girls I thought I was impressing. I lost to a guy who did magic tricks as he danced, and I soon realized I was only a fine dancer compared to a bunch of drunk people at an accounting department's Christmas party and that I would not be taking over as John Travolta's dance double anytime soon.

Now that I've set the '70s scene, let's talk about the Harvey Wallbanger, one of the most famous disco-era drinks. Since they didn't serve booze at my teen disco and since disco was officially dead by the time I was old enough to order one, I never had a Harvey Wallbanger in its heyday. All I knew was that the name made me laugh and it sounded like a drink you'd be very cool ordering.

Only recently did I investigate what was in the drink, and it was pretty disappointing, frankly. In my imagination it was a very involved drink, filled with so many different liquors that you'd end the night drunkenly banging your head against a wall. But it's pretty much just a screwdriver with some Galliano floating on top of it. I think they squandered a cool name on a simple drink. If you're banging your head against a wall after drinking vodka and orange juice, then you really shouldn't be drinking.

All that said, it's actually a really good drink, and sort of fun to make because of the Galliano float, and it's always going to sound great when you hand somebody a glass and say, "Here, it's a Harvey Wallbanger." So, hit the wall!

FILL a Tom Collins glass with ice and add the vodka and orange juice. Stir the drink, then float the Galliano on top of it by pouring it slowly over the back of a bar spoon without mixing it in. Garnish with a cherry and orange slice on a cocktail pick, then turn the beat around and bang it down!

COCKTAIL #34—CAPRI COCKTAIL

The song—"Baila Morena" by Zucchero

Ice

¾ ounce crème de cacao (light)

¾ ounce crème de banane

¾ ounce light cream or milk

Tipsy's and my favorite place in the world is the Isle of Capri off the coast of Naples, Italy. We started going there in the mid-'90s and haven't missed a year there yet. To us, it's like heaven on earth. A lot of people you talk to who have been there say, "It's not that great, it's just a lot of tourists." This is true if you take the ferry in the morning and walk around for a few hours with all the other tourists who come in for the day and then leave before the sun goes down. Because you're simply walking around in the heat of the day with a bunch of people who are just sightseeing and looking for lunch.

No, Capri is the place where you get a hotel room, sleep in late, and hang out around the pool all day while the tourists are packing the streets and cafés, and then when the last ferry leaves, you put on your nice clothes and head into town for drinks, dinner, and strolling. You have an amazing meal at a restaurant like Aurora or Le Grottelle or Da Paolino, and then you walk over to the Quisisana Hotel and get a table on the patio bar and order a couple of spritzes and watch the rich yacht owners and the stylish locals stroll past in their finest vacation evening wear. Maybe you go to one of the nightclubs and dance to the live bands playing Italian pop classics, or maybe you head up to Anacapri and have another drink on the patio of the Caesar Augustus Hotel, which overlooks the entire island, or maybe you shop in some of the nice stores that are open late, or maybe you even stop by the Isaia store and have a drink with Gianluca Isaia and Giulia Natale on the back patio while

Gianluca smokes and plays old Neapolitan classics from his iPhone and you dance the night away surrounded by all the amazing clothes he designs and sells. Then you go back to your room and sleep soundly and get up the next morning and do it all again.

That's how you do Capri.

Well, this drink reminds Tipsy and me of all those things. It's definitely more of a dessert drink, but since your time on Capri is all about *la dolce vita*—the sweet life—this sweet drink says all that and more. So mix one up, take a sip, and imagine you're on that shining gem of an island off the Amalfi Coast. *Saluti!*

FILL a cocktail shaker with ice and add the crème de cacao, crème de banane, and cream or milk. Shake and strain into an old fashioned glass with fresh ice cubes. Capri's calling!

COCKTAIL #35—HOT PANTS!

The song—"Love Train" by the O'Jays

Margarita salt or coarse kosher salt

Ice

1½ ounces tequila

½ ounce peppermint schnapps

½ ounce fresh grapefruit juice

1 teaspoon powdered sugar

Okay, I'm not going to lie. This drink is awful. It's so awful that it's now the punchline to a lot of jokes in our house. The story behind this drink? It was our friend the great actress/comedian/singer Bridget Everett's birthday and I wanted to dedicate that day's cocktail show to her. I asked her what drink she wanted me to make, and she said anything with tequila. Having just done margaritas a week earlier and wanting to surprise her with something unexpected, I took to my *Mr. Boston* book and started looking through all the tequila recipes.

If you know Bridget Everett, you know her nightclub act is very funny and very bawdy. So when I discovered a tequila drink called a Hot Pants, I thought I had found the Holy Grail. It had the tequila Bridget wanted, but it was packaged with a hilarious name and had a history as another famous disco-era drink. What could be more perfect?

Well, one look at the recipe should tell you we were headed for disaster. On their own, they're all good ingredients. And this was *Mr. Boston*, the trusty old guide for bartenders. Even though it didn't look like a drink that would work, I figured there had to be some genius magic involved, various properties that each ingredient would bring out or suppress in the other ingredients. This was going to be alchemy, pure and simple. I was sure of it.

As you already know, it wasn't. It was four ingredients stuffed into a glass like murderous clowns who got trapped in a tiny car and each decided to kill one another. One sip was an assault on the senses. If I had to pick the most psychopathic clown in the car, it would be the peppermint schnapps. It's a good drink to have in a flask at a college football game when you're sitting out in the snow freezing your ass off, but in a glass with tequila and grapefruit and a little sugar in it, it is definitely the odd man out. And *then* you're asked to rim the glass with salt, just to make sure there's not one taste bud on your tongue that isn't offended!

All this said, I would like to invite you to experience a Hot Pants. I say this because this was a drink that people apparently used to enjoy. It wouldn't have been in that *Mr. Boston* book if it wasn't. Maybe its fans were all whacked out on cocaine because it was the late '70s. Maybe that drug deadened your taste buds so much that they needed to be jolted awake by one of the worst combinations of booze ever to coexist in a glass.

Or maybe some people just like it. Maybe I'm just a snob. Maybe you're one of the people who will like this drink. I'm not here to judge. If this became your new favorite cocktail, I would be thrilled. But you won't know until you try! Good luck! I'm pulling for you.

And I'm sorry, Bridget. I'll make it up to you on your next birthday.

WET the rim of an old fashioned glass and dip it in a plate of the salt. Set aside, then fill a cocktail shaker with ice and add the tequila, schnapps, grapefruit juice, and powdered sugar. Shake and strain into the salt-rimmed glass. Sip and . . . enjoy??? You never know!

COCKTAIL #36—WHISKEY SOUR

The song—"Ain't That a Kick in the Head" by Dean Martin

Ice

2 ounces rye whiskey or bourbon

1 ounce fresh lemon juice (see Note)

¾ ounce simple syrup (page 112) or maple syrup

Cocktail cherry

Lemon twist

There's not much to say about this one. It's a classic. It's now one of my favorite cocktails. And yet I put off trying one for the longest time. Why? The word *sour*.

It's one of the most complicated words in the English language. Or at least it is to me. In my house growing up, my dad loved things that had the word *sour* in them. Sour cream, sauerkraut (which I always thought was "sour kraut," and it may as well have been, because that's how it tasted), Sour Patch Kids candy. Okay, he didn't love Sour Patch Kids candy, but my friends did. And everything I ate that had the word *sour* in it tasted terrible to me.

So it was only natural that I wouldn't be drawn to a drink with *sour* in the name. But when I started making cocktails, I read the recipe and thought, *Hey, that actually sounds pretty good.* Whiskey, lemon juice, and simple syrup—how bad could that be? And it wasn't bad. It was great. And it has become a drink I make myself all the time.

Now, some recipes for whiskey sours include an egg white and others don't. If you remember all the way back to the gin sour we made, that had egg white and it was delicious. A whiskey sour with an egg white is delicious and creamy, too. And yet I really like it without the egg.

First, it's much easier and quicker to make sans egg. Second, you don't have to feel guilty about wasting an egg yolk or trying to save it for some future baking project that you'll probably never do. And last but certainly not least, I just like the taste of the whiskey with the sweet and sour mixture, which is basically what lemon juice and simple syrup is. Whenever I can keep things uncomplicated, I'm happy.

A classic sour is usually presented in a sour glass (sort of a cross between a martini glass and a small wineglass) and served with no ice. That works better when you're doing the egg white version, because the layer of foam on top makes it look more like a fancy cocktail. It also calls for a bit of club soda. But I like a very simple sour and so I have mine in an old fashioned glass on the rocks with no club soda. It makes it a bit more tart, aka sour, but in this drink, I like that. You can even substitute maple syrup for the simple syrup, which gives it an even richer sweetness within the sour.

One other tip is to use rye whiskey if you can. I love Templeton Rye and even recommend using their more expensive six-year-old if you can swing it. Having good whiskey or bourbon in a whiskey sour makes a difference. It cuts through the sweet and sour enough to keep its character. And don't we all want to keep our character intact through all the sweet and sour that we go through in life? Poetic, huh? Okay, here's how to make one . . .

FILL a cocktail shaker with ice, add the rye or bourbon, lemon juice, and syrup, and shake. Pour the mixture into an old fashioned glass, ice and all. Add a few more ice cubes to fill the glass, then garnish with a cherry and a lemon twist. Step into the sour life!

NOTE: You can also try ½ ounce lemon juice and ½ ounce lime juice for some added flavor and fun.

There's now a cool vegan egg white substitute that you can use if you don't want to break any eggs at your bar. It's called Ms. Better's Bitters Miraculous Foamer, and all you do is squirt one-third of a dropper of it into your shaker and shake your cocktail as normal. It gives you a beautiful head of foam without cracking a shell. Miraculous is right!

IF YOU WANT FOAM BUT NO EGGS

COCKTAIL #37—THE JUPITER

The song—"Neutron Dance" by the Pointer Sisters

Ice

1½ ounces gin

¾ ounce dry vermouth

1 teaspoon Parfait Amour liqueur

1 teaspoon fresh orange juice

There are several reasons I like this drink. First, I'm an astronomy nerd, so I like that it's named after a planet in our solar system. (When I was a teen, I wanted to be an astronomer because I thought I could look for UFOs for a living. Then I found out you need to be good at math and so quickly gave up that dream.) Second, it comes from Ted Haigh, aka Dr. Cocktail, and every old recipe he finds is great. And third, this was the drink that began the never-ending expansion of my bar from sane to insane.

I wrote earlier about how the deeper you get into mixology, the more your collection of bottles will grow. Well, this was the first drink I made that used an ingredient I'd never heard of before, Parfait Amour. It's a liqueur made of sweet oranges, orange blossoms, and vanilla pods that is colored to give it a mauve-blue tint. In this cocktail, the purplish blue hue mixes with the orange juice to become a lovely lavender color, making the drink quite pretty and elegant. It's a drink that looks and sounds like it's going to be sweet, but it actually has a nice, slightly bitter edge to it from the Parfait Amour. Ted says that it's not a timid liqueur, and he's right, so we both advise you not to overpour the Amour.

Try this delicious drink and you'll want to impress all your friends with it. And *that's* amore!

FILL a cocktail shaker with ice, add all the ingredients, and shake and strain into a chilled cocktail glass. Blast off!

COCKTAIL #38—PARK AVENUE

The song—"Jump, Jive an' Wail" by Louis Prima

Ice

2 ounces gin

¾ ounce pineapple juice

¾ ounce sweet vermouth

2 teaspoons orange Curaçao

I love New York City. Tipsy and I have a small apartment there, and every chance I get I go to the Big Apple to write and to eat at my most beloved restaurants and drink at my favorite bars. Our apartment is between Madison Avenue and Park Avenue. It's a short walk to what I think is the greatest American bar, Bemelmans Bar in the Carlyle Hotel. My perfect evening out is to eat at Ralph Lauren's Polo Bar or Il Tinello Italian restaurant and then walk down to Bemelmans and sit at my favorite table right next to the piano. There are always wonderful musicians like Loston Harris and Earl Rose playing great American songbook standards from the likes of Cole Porter and George Gershwin, and it's just the best grown-up evening in the world.

So when I found this recipe with such a quintessentially New York name, I just had to try it. It's really a great one. The mix of pineapple and orange liqueur interacting with the sweet vermouth and gin creates a drink that is fruity but not overly sweet. It's simply a crowd-pleaser that I would feel confident serving even to people who say they don't like gin. The other three ingredients don't bury the gin but instead show it off at its finest, rounding its edges while letting it keep its junipery voice. So take a stroll down Park Avenue with this tasty tipple!

FILL a cocktail shaker with ice and add the rest of the ingredients. Shake and strain into a chilled cocktail glass. Take a sip of the Big Apple!

COCKTAIL #39—BANANA DAIQUIRI

The song—"Monkey Man" by the Specials

Ice

2 ounces rum

½ ounce crème de banane

1 ounce fresh lime juice

¼ ounce simple syrup (page 112)

Banana slice

Oooh baby, this drink is a good one. It's probably more of a dessert drink, though, to be honest. The interplay between the crème de banane and the lime juice gives it a tartness that the simple syrup then sweetens up. I'd start lighter on the simple syrup and maybe even mix it first without any, then taste it to see if you think it needs more sweetness. You can always put in more simple syrup, but you can't take it out once it's in, so experiment to find your perfect mix. That's the fun of mixology. The recipe is there to let you know the ingredients and the basic proportions, but you can play with the amounts, because everybody's tastes are different.

So *vive la différence* and banana it up!

FILL a cocktail shaker with ice and add the rum, crème de banane, lime juice, and simple syrup. Shake and strain into a chilled coupe or cocktail glass. (You can also enjoy it in an old fashioned glass on the rocks—up to you.) Garnish with a banana slice and go bananas!

COCKTAIL #40—THE SQUEAKY DOOR

ANOTHER PAUL FEIG ORIGINAL

The song—"Katmandu" by Bob Seger

Ice

1½ ounces gin

½ ounce cherry liqueur (preferably Cherry Heering)

½ ounce orange Curaçao

½ ounce St. Germain elderflower liqueur

2 dashes of cherry bitters

Juice from half a lemon

Club soda

Cocktail cherry

Lemon twist

I couldn't be prouder of this drink I invented. The story behind it is this:

When I was doing my *Quarantine Cocktail Time!* shows, Tipsy would always come in toward the end to say hi and try whatever cocktail I made. My home bar is in the guesthouse we have in our backyard, and the door to it hasn't been oiled in years, so whenever it opens or closes, it squeaks like crazy. Like "in a haunted house" crazy. And so our loyal viewers always knew when Laurie was coming in because they'd hear this long, loud squeak. I started referring to the sound of "the squeaky door" to announce her arrival, and soon people began writing in the comments that I should invent a drink called the Squeaky Door. I thought it was such a good idea, and I loved the thought of honoring my wife of twenty-nine-plus years with her very own cocktail.

And thus the Squeaky Door was invented.

I started with ingredients I knew she liked from other drinks I had made and figured out the best way to combine them. Since the drink features several liqueurs that are on the sweeter side, I knew I needed to add lemon and club soda to cut back on the sweetness. The result is a drink I'm not only proud of and love to drink, but one that has actually gotten a bit of a following. Redbird, the great restaurant and bar in downtown Los Angeles, even partnered with Artingstall's to put out a bottled version of it for people to drink at home, along with whatever delicious takeout they ordered from this amazing restaurant.

So here it is, my boozy ode to my tipsy wife, for your bartending enjoyment. Ladies and gentlemen, I give you . . . the Squeaky Door!

FILL a cocktail shaker with ice and add the gin, cherry liqueur, Curaçao, St. Germain, bitters, and lemon juice. Shake and strain into an ice-filled Tom Collins glass. Top with club soda and garnish with a cherry and a lemon twist. The perfect way to grease your squeaky wheel!

COCKTAIL #41—THE BRONX

The song—"I'm a Man" by the Spencer Davis Group

Ice

1½ ounces gin

¾ ounce sweet vermouth

¾ ounce dry vermouth

Juice of ¼ orange

Dash of orange bitters (optional)

A Bronx cheer is something you do to show disapproval. But a Bronx cocktail is something you make to show somebody how much you like them! Or so says me. Every ingredient in this drink is delightful, and when you mix them all together, they get even delightfuller. And yes, *delightfuller* is a word. Along with *delightfullest*. Are they really? Sure, why the heck not? It's my book. I can do whatever I want. I'm the captain now!

Okay, sorry. I got a little carried away. They're not words. But it *is* my book. And this drink is delightful, delightfuller, and delightfullest. You be the judge, but—I have a feeling you'll agree with me!

FILL a cocktail shaker with ice and add the gin, vermouths, orange juice, and bitters, if using. Shake and strain into a chilled coupe or cocktail glass. Three cheers for the Bronx!

COCKTAIL #42—TURQUOISE DAIQUIRI

The song—"Goody Two Shoes" by Adam Ant

Ice

1 ounce light rum

½ ounce Cointreau orange liqueur or triple sec

½ ounce blue Curaçao

1 ounce fresh lime juice

1½ ounces pineapple juice

I'd never had Curaçao, blue or otherwise, before I started doing my cocktail show. I was such a Curaçao novice that I didn't even know how to pronounce it. It was only after several shows-worth of mispronunciations that I was guided to the proper pronunciation by some of our more patient viewers. My pronunciation hint now is that when you have a sick pig, you have to *cure-a-sow*. And now you'll never mispronounce it either.

Regular Curaçao is golden in color and delightfully orange in flavor. So when I discovered that blue Curaçao tastes basically the same as regular Curaçao but looks way more fun because of its awesome 2000 Flushes hue, I realized how much flash it could add to certain drinks. After all, a delicious cocktail is great, but if it jumps out at your eye, then all the better.

The Turquoise Daiquiri demands attention and always brings a smile to your face. When I was growing up, our local ice cream parlor used to serve Blue Moon ice cream, and we all thought it was the greatest thing ever because it tasted wonderful and also turned your tongue blue. While the Turquoise Daiquiri won't give you a blue tongue, it will intrigue the adult in you, because . . . well . . . it's boozy and delicious! Give it a whirl. The only thing that won't be blue is you!

FILL a cocktail shaker with ice and add the rest of the ingredients. Shake, strain into a chilled martini glass, and sip away. The turquoise way!

COCKTAIL #43—BRANDY ALEXANDER

The song—"Real Wild Child" by Iggy Pop

Ice

1 ounce brandy

1 ounce dark crème de cacao

1 ounce heavy cream (or light cream or half-and-half)

Whole nutmeg seed

My obsession with cream-based dessert drinks started with the Brandy Alexander. But at first it was an obsession of derision. I remember hearing it mentioned in old movies and TV shows when I was growing up, and it was always positioned as a cocktail that old ladies drank, so it became a bit of a punchline for me.

And then I made one.

Any drinks made with heavy cream are dicey for a couple of reasons. First, if you're lactose intolerant, then fire in the hole! Second, they're not at all dietetic. So you need to make sure people know what's in one of these before you serve it. Some people will turn it down, like folks who don't want cream in their soup, but those who don't reject it will really go nuts. Why? Because it's so damn good!

Cream-based cocktails are like drinking the most delicious cold melted ice cream in the world. They make everyone happy, even cocktail purists who normally turn up their noses at dessert drinks. It helps that the Brandy Alexander has been around for quite a while and has some history to legitimize it. But mostly it's an insanely delicious drink that tastes like a dessert but is boozy enough to feel like a cocktail.

Do we dare call it a grown-up treat? Of course we do! Now see for yourself . . .

FILL a cocktail shaker with ice and add the brandy, crème de cacao, and cream. Shake and strain into a chilled cocktail glass. Grate fresh nutmeg on top. The sailors say, "Brandy, you're a fine drink!"

COCKTAIL #44—MAMBO!

The song—"Mambo No. 5" by Lou Bega

Ice

1 ounce gin or vodka

1 ounce Cointreau orange liqueur or triple sec

1 ounce apricot brandy

¼ ounce Italian bitter aperitivo (Campari, Select, or another)

2½ ounces fresh orange juice

½ ounce orange Curaçao

When we made *Freaks and Geeks*, we had a launch party for the show at a bowling alley in Los Angeles. There was a dance club in the bar, and during the evening I wandered in and found some of our cast members there. Suddenly, a song I had never heard before came on, and Linda Cardellini and Busy Philipps jumped out of their chairs and onto the dance floor. The song was so much fun and so full of energy, and Linda and Busy were dancing wildly and having the greatest time.

I asked Samm Levine what the song was, and he said, "'Mambo Number Five' by Blue Vega.'" Or that's what I thought he said. I spent the next week trying to find albums from Blue Vega and had no luck at all. When I finally figured out the song was by Lou Bega, I felt like a real dummy. But I'll never forget the fun and infectious energy Linda and Busy had when they were dancing to that song.

Well, the Mambo is the perfect embodiment of that song and that experience. It practically jumps out of the glass and dances on your tongue. It's like a vacation in the sun. It's fun, it's fresh, and it makes you feel good. It's boozy enough to feel like a cocktail yet fruity enough to distract you from the fact that there's a lot of alcohol in your glass. In short, it's a really great drink that may very well send you to the dance floor. One way or another!

FILL a cocktail shaker with ice and add all the ingredients. Shake and strain into an ice-filled Collins or highball glass. Mambo number one!

COCKTAIL #45—FRENCH 75

The song—"Ça s'est Arrangé" by Jean-Paul Keller

For a few years there was a restaurant near our house in Burbank called French 75, and we used to eat there all the time. I had no idea what the name meant, but the food was great and it was a very nice place. I didn't learn the meaning until I went to a fancy party that our friend Pam Harper was throwing in London a few years later. A waiter came around with a tray of drinks and said, "Would you like a French 75?" I went, "Hey, that's the name of a restaurant by my house!" The waiter nodded politely and walked away, probably wondering what this dumb American was doing at a high-class British party.

But he handed me one of the glasses before he walked away, and I tasted my first French 75. It would not be my last. It's a delicious blend of gin, Champagne, and lemon juice with a bit of sweetener, and it all seems like it shouldn't work. However, it *really* works. It was named after a 75mm Pack Howitzer field gun used in World War I that was famous for its accuracy and the kick that it made when it fired. This drink has that kick, hence the name. You don't realize it at first, and so it's easy to knock back several of these thinking you're just enjoying a refreshing bubbly beverage. Then, wham! The kick of the 75.

Now, here are my Drunk Funcle tips to make this the best drink ever:

Tip #1—Chill your glass in the freezer for at least 10 minutes before you pour your drink into it. Prepare everything, even opening the Champagne, before you take the glass out. It should be ice-cold and frosty, and you should pour your drink right from your shaker into the frozen glass, then top with the Champagne and enjoy it immediately. Otherwise the frost will melt and it won't be the extra cold that makes it extra good.

Tip #2—Try substituting a mild honey in place of the simple syrup or sugar. It adds a nice round quality to the drink and feels just the tiniest bit healthier. Of course, this is an illusion, because you're still drinking gin and Champagne, but, hey, I'm all for anything that alleviates guilt! Just make sure to stir the honey with the gin and lemon juice long enough to dissolve it. Do this before you add the ice so you know the honey has broken down, then add the ice and proceed.

Now, go pop open a bottle of champers, squeeze some lemons, and get French with your new favorite drink!

Ice

2 ounces gin

1 ounce fresh lemon juice

1 teaspoon simple syrup (page 112) or 2 teaspoons sugar (or 1 teaspoon honey, as mentioned above)

Champagne or sparkling wine

Long lemon peel

FILL a cocktail shaker with ice and add the gin, lemon juice, and simple syrup or honey. Shake and strain into a very chilled Champagne flute. Top with Champagne and garnish with a long lemon twist. Ka-blam!

COCKTAIL #46—MAI TAI (THE VERY SWEET VERSION)

The song—"My Sharona" by the Knack

Crushed ice

1 ounce light rum

1 ounce dark rum

½ ounce orange Curaçao

1½ ounces simple syrup (page 112)

1½ ounces orgeat syrup

Lime peel

Mint sprig

Sometimes drinks don't come out the way you think they will. I had never tried a Mai Tai before my cocktail show, and I wasn't sure what to expect. I also didn't have orgeat in my home bar, so I had to order this sweet almond syrup and it took forever to arrive. When it finally did, I was so excited to make this drink that I could hardly contain myself.

I mixed it up on my show, and Tipsy and I each took a taste. It was really sweet. Like, *really* sweet. I don't mind a sweet drink, as you can tell from some of the drinks I've invented. But occasionally you'll come across a drink whose sweetness is so far forward that it wipes out all the other tastes in the glass.

So if you like your drinks on the very sweet side, give this recipe a whirl. And if you'd rather have a more traditional (and delicious) Mai Tai, you'll find the original Trader Vic's recipe on page 214. You can also start by just using a ½ ounce of orgeat and a ½ ounce of simple syrup and see if you want to make the drink sweeter by adding the extra ounce of each. Totally up to you.

Here's to the (really really) sweet life!

FILL a cocktail shaker with crushed ice and add the rums, Curaçao, simple syrup, and orgeat. Shake and strain into an old fashioned or Tom Collins glass over fresh ice. Garnish with a lime peel and a mint sprig. Sa-weet!!!

COCKTAIL #47—FRESH PINEAPPLE MARGARITAS

The song—"Pehli Baar" by Sukriti Kakar and Siddharth Mahadevan

1½ cups diced fresh pineapple (½ pound)

½ cup fresh lime juice

½ cup tequila blanco

¼ cup Cointreau orange liqueur or triple sec

Lime wedges

Margarita salt or coarse kosher salt

MAKES 2 COCKTAILS

We've already talked about the marvel that is pineapple juice, so imagine a drink with a whole pineapple shoved into it. Well, after it's been put through a blender, that is. Delicious!

I'm not a huge fan of blender drinks because I don't like having that big piece of equipment on my bar, and I also really enjoy shaking and stirring drinks. A blender takes all that fun away, and you're left as a casual observer watching a machine have all the fun.

But once that machine stops and you pour out a smooth, blended margarita, your irrational jealousy toward an inanimate device that exists only to make your life easier abates and you slip into a world of delight. Or at least mine does.

Don't believe me? Well, then get yourself a fresh pineapple from the pineapple store (do they have those?), cut it up, and make it happen!!!

COMBINE the pineapple, lime juice, tequila, and Cointreau or triple sec in a blender and pulse until smooth. Wet the rims of 2 margarita glasses with a lime wedge and then dip the rims in a dish of salt. Divide the margarita mixture between the 2 glasses and garnish each cocktail with a lime wedge. As Kristen Wiig said in *Bridesmaids*, "Shit, that is fresh!"

COCKTAIL #48—THE BLUE MOON

The Song—"Flash Light" by Parliament

Ice

2 ounces gin

½ ounce crème de violette

½ ounce fresh lemon juice

Lemon twist

Besides being an astronomy nerd, I'm also a sci-fi nerd, so I first found this drink for my "May the Fourth Be with You" episode of *Quarantine Cocktail Time!* It made me think of *Star Wars* because of the famous Obi-Wan Kenobi line when he sees the Death Star: "That's no moon." I also was at the height of my love of acquiring bottles of what I considered to be obscure liqueurs, and crème de violette (also known as crème Yvette in some circles) checked that box, too. I also just thought it looked like a pretty drink. (You'll begin to notice my weird obsession with blue drinks as you go through this book. I don't know where it came from. Purple is my favorite color; I'm not even a particular fan of blue. But turn a drink blue and something goes haywire in my brain.) Tipsy says this drink tastes like candy, so it's definitely on the slightly sweeter side because of the crème de violette. But the lemon juice does a nice job of taking that edge off, so it's a delightfully smooth cocktail to impress your friends with.

There's also something so elegant about three-ingredient drinks, and once you have the ingredients on hand, this is an incredibly easy one to make. The combination of ease and uniqueness here make this a solid bet for your regular cocktail lineup.

May the Blue Moon be with you!

FILL a cocktail shaker with ice and add the gin, crème de violette, and lemon juice. Shake and strain into a chilled cocktail glass. Garnish with a lemon twist. We have liftoff!

COCKTAIL #49—ROB W. ROY

ANOTHER PAUL FEIG ORIGINAL

The song—"Livin' la Vida Loca" by Ricky Martin

Ice

2 ounces scotch whisky

¾ ounce sweet vermouth

¾ ounce orange Curaçao

2 dashes of orange bitters

Cocktail cherry

My friend Rob Watzke and I thought the name Rob Roy for a cocktail was hilarious when we were in our twenties. I have no idea why other than it was fun to pretend to order the drink in a deep, Cliff the mailman from *Cheers* voice, "Bartender, I'll have a *Rob Roy*." It was funnier in person than it is on the page. Or maybe it wasn't funny at all. But it still made us laugh.

We were nerds. What can I say?

In many ways, a Rob Roy is just a Manhattan. It has a bit more sweet vermouth than a Manhattan, and it's occasionally served on the rocks, but that's basically it. So I thought it would be fun to put a bit of a spin on it, and since this drink is so connected in my brain to my friend Rob Watzke, I decided to dedicate it to him. Hence: the Rob W. Roy.

My inspiration for this variation was an old fashioned, since it's also a scotch-based drink with something sweet in it. In the case of the old fashioned, the sweetener is sugar. But you also float an orange slice in it, so I thought I could pull back on the scotch and sweet vermouth a bit to make room for my good friend Curaçao. And that's exactly what I did. I also made this into a rocks drink, again like an old fashioned.

And now I will immodestly say that the result is really good. Score one for Feig. But I'll leave that for you to decide.

Without further ado, I give you the Rob W. Roy!

FILL a mixing glass with ice, add the scotch, vermouth, Curaçao, and bitters, and stir until cold. Pour it all into an old fashioned glass, adding more ice if necessary to fill the glass. Garnish with a cocktail cherry and enjoy your Roy!

AND for any of you traditionalists who want to make a proper Rob Roy, here's that recipe:

ROB ROY (THE TRADITIONAL WAY)

Ice
2½ ounces scotch whisky
1 ounce sweet vermouth

2 dashes of orange bitters
Cocktail cherry

FILL a mixing glass with ice, add the scotch, vermouth, and bitters, and stir until cold. Strain into a chilled cocktail glass or over fresh ice in an old fashioned glass. Garnish with a cocktail cherry. It's no Feig original, but it's still pretty darn tasty!

COCKTAIL #50—SATAN'S WHISKERS

The song—"Hey Ya!" by OutKast

Ice

½ ounce gin

½ ounce dry vermouth

½ ounce sweet vermouth

½ ounce fresh orange juice

2 teaspoons orange Curaçao or Grand Marnier orange liqueur

1 teaspoon orange bitters

Long, thin, curly orange twist

For a drink with such an evil name, this drink is surprisingly friendly. But maybe that's why it sounds like it's the work of the devil. You don't realize just what it's doing to you as you're drinking it. It definitely goes down smooth. So I guess you could say it's devilishly good! Yes, I went there. Low-hanging fruit, and I'm always ready to pick it.

When I made this on our fiftieth episode of *Quarantine Cocktail Time!*, we had only blood oranges in the house, so I used those for the juice part of the recipe. I have to say, they made it a really great drink. Obviously regular oranges are fine, but if you're lucky enough to get your hands on some blood oranges, give them a try. They make the drink an even more evil color! Take a trip to the dark, delicious side!

FILL a cocktail shaker with ice and add the gin, vermouths, orange juice, Curaçao, and bitters. Shake and strain into a chilled cocktail glass. Garnish with the long orange twist. Because that's Satan's whisker! This is one hell of a good drink! Yes, I went there again.

COCKTAIL #51—TOP BANANA

The song—"Go Bananas" by Little Big

Ice

1 ounce vodka
or Artingstall's
Brilliant London
Dry Gin

1 ounce crème
de banane

Juice of half
an orange
(about 1 ounce)

I used to get calf cramps all the time when I was younger. I'd be comfortably sound asleep in bed, then drowsily wake up and have a nice lazy stretch, only to have my leg seize up in a horrendous cramp that felt like my calf muscle had suddenly transformed into a softball. After the pain and adrenaline rush passed, I'd be wide awake the rest of the night and tired the next day, and, to top it all off, my leg would still be sore.

Yes, calf cramps are the worst. They come from a potassium deficiency. How do you help get rid of them? You eat bananas, which are high in potassium. But what if you drink a cocktail that features banana liqueur? Will that cure cramps, too? No! Of course not. What's wrong with you? But nice try, you boozer.

This is a simple little drink. There's something about the banana and orange flavors that makes it seem like an after-dinner treat, but it's not sweet.

The Top Banana works with both vodka or a very dry gin, like Artingstall's. Any gin with a strong juniper taste will compete too much with the fruitiness of the other ingredients, but a light, slightly citrusy gin will bring an extra touch of complexity to an otherwise simple drink.

So eat a banana to make sure you get a good night's sleep, then cap it off with a delicious Top Banana! It'll a-peel to you. Pow! (Yes, odds are good that I'm going to keep making puns. I'll just stop apologizing now.)

FILL a cocktail shaker with ice and add the vodka or gin, crème de banane, and orange juice. Shake and strain into an old fashioned glass over fresh ice. Prepare for a banana-rama!

COCKTAIL #52—CHURCHILL MANHATTAN

The song—"All Day and All of the Night" by the Kinks

Tipsy and I lived in London for a year when I was making the movie *Last Christmas*. We were in heaven because we lived in beautiful Mayfair, the heart of classic London, right across the street from Hyde Park. The film shot all through the winter and was never rained out once, which was a miracle for rainy old London. So you could say the movie gods were on our side.

It was very cold at this time, but any day that I could, I would walk up Mount Street past the Connaught Hotel and continue on to my favorite hotel in the world, Claridge's, to have breakfast. On my way, I would pass a cigar store called Sautter Cigars. They always had lots of Winston Churchill memorabilia in their front window because, well, Churchill clearly loved cigars.

One day as I walked past, I noticed a sign in their window that read, "Winston Churchill once lived in the apartment above this store." I was so surprised. But London's interesting that way. As you walk around any neighborhood, you'll see blue plaques on houses that tell you about all manner of famous people who once lived there. Writers, actors, politicians—they're everywhere.

Our good friend the hilarious Australian novelist Kathy Lette used to take us to one of Churchill's favorite restaurants, Simpson's, right next to the Savoy Hotel on the Strand. (We actually shot a scene from *Last Christmas* in front of Simpson's, when Emilia Clarke and Henry Golding talk on a bench after an ice-skating date.) Kathy is such a regular there that she would always get us the Winston Churchill table, where he used to eat all the time, which is in the back corner and overlooks the entire restaurant. And it was in the bar at the Savoy right next door where the Churchill Manhattan was invented for Mr. Churchill himself.

The Churchill Manhattan is an incredibly tasty drink that even people who don't like scotch (Tipsy) will like. (She did.) The introduction of the orangey Cointreau and the tart lime juice softens the standard scotch-forward Manhattan, with the bonus of making it an incredibly pretty drink.

But don't just take my word for it. Mix yourself up a Churchill Manhattan and defend your bar against boring cocktails!

Ice

1½ ounces scotch whisky

½ ounce sweet vermouth

½ ounce Cointreau orange liqueur

½ ounce fresh lime juice

FILL a mixing glass with ice and add all the ingredients. Stir and strain into a chilled cocktail glass. Never never never give up . . . enjoying this drink!

COCKTAIL #53—SAUCY SUE

The song—"Saturday Night" by Bay City Rollers

Ice

2 ounces Calvados apple brandy

¼ ounce apricot brandy

¼ ounce Pernod or other pastis

Lemon twist

The word *saucy* has always cracked me up. My friend the British actor and writer Morwenna Banks made me laugh heartily once when she told me that as a kid she invented a song called "Cyril the Saucy Snake." And when I run across a drink with a name that makes me laugh, I'm going to make it. Whether it's a good idea or not.

This is a strong drink. It's also an odd drink. Some may not like it. Others will. With two different kinds of brandy and then some pastis thrown in for good measure, it's a drink with a lot going on. Perhaps too much going on. But I'll let you be the judge. The one thing I can say for sure is that this cocktail definitely lives up to its name. They don't get much saucier than this!

FILL a mixing glass with ice and add the apple brandy, apricot brandy, and Pernod. Stir and strain into a chilled cocktail glass. Add a lemon twist. Hit this sauce!

COCKTAIL #54—GRASSHOPPER

The song—"Sex Bomb" by Tom Jones

Ice

1 ounce green
crème de menthe

1 ounce white
crème de cacao

2 ounces heavy
cream

Whole nutmeg
seed

I directed an episode in the first season of *Mad Men*. At that time, I was wearing mostly 1960s-style suits with thin lapels and thin ties that I had picked up in thrift stores or bought new from Ralph Lauren's Black Label line, which had that same midcentury cut. The style fit my love of all things cool from the 1950s and '60s. It was a Rat Pack–Bobby Darin–Lenny Bruce look that I thought (and still think) makes most guys look great.

When my agent sent me the pilot of *Mad Men* to see if I'd want to direct an episode, I loved it because it was about that era, and the aesthetics reflected the way I liked to dress and wished the world still looked like. So I said I'd love to be involved. I went to the studio dressed in a suit, as I always am, and headed in to meet Matt Weiner, the show's creator and executive producer.

When I told his assistant I had an appointment, she looked at me and said, "Oh, casting is down the hall." She thought I was an actor who had dressed up like the characters on the show in order to get hired. In the years after that, when I would wear my suits, people constantly said to me, "Oh, so you're a fan of *Mad Men*, huh?" Which drove me crazy. It was my style long before the show, but now I just looked like I was doing *Mad Men* cosplay. So I abandoned that style and all those suits and went back to wider lapels and slightly looser fits but kept a chip on my shoulder about it. When you have to get rid of that many suits, you have to blame someone.

So, why did I tell you all this? Because to me a Grasshopper is the epitome of a drink from that era. It conjures up images of the women from Slim Aarons photos sitting around sunlit swimming pools sipping from martini glasses filled with this mint-green creamy delight, smoking cigarettes, wearing boldly colored fashions, and occasionally getting up to dance the twist to French and Italian pop songs.

Sure, I'm running a few eras together, but it's my mental image and I'm sticking with it.

Whatever images it conjures up for you, I can tell you that this drink is an absolute crowd-pleaser. I've never made one for anybody who said they didn't like it. Simply put, people flip over it, and I guarantee you and your guests will flip over it, too, when you make this delicious creamy cocktail! Hop to it!

FILL a cocktail shaker with ice and add the crème de menthe, crème de cacao, and heavy cream. Shake vigorously and strain into a chilled cocktail glass. Grate fresh nutmeg on top and jump for joy!

COCKTAIL #55—AVIATION

The song—"I Can't Drive 55" by Sammy Hagar

Ice

2 ounces gin

½ ounce
maraschino cherry
liqueur

¼ ounce crème de
violette

¾ ounce fresh
lemon juice

Lemon twist

Cilantro is loved by some people and hated by others. And so is the Aviation cocktail! It's an old drink that couldn't be found in the United States for a long time because crème de violette wasn't available. But then someone started importing it, and the drink took off. For a while, at least. Then it fell out of favor once more.

You may remember our good friend crème de violette from the Blue Moon cocktail (page 156). It works very well in that but for some reason is trickier in an Aviation. The recipe from *The Savoy Cocktail Book* doesn't even include crème de violette. Some cocktail purists still like the crème-free version, with a few saying that the violette version tastes like dish soap. But other civilians I know absolutely love the Aviation. So, as with all things in life, it's down to personal taste, just like cilantro.

I've come across a few variations on this recipe and definitely agree that it's wise to approach crème de violette cautiously. Some recipes call for a half ounce of both maraschino liqueur (a tricky ingredient in its own right) and crème de violette. I made a classic Aviation on my show, and Tipsy found it a bit too much. So, I've scaled back the crème de violette in this recipe but left the maraschino as is. But play around to find your perfect combo.

Jump into the cockpit and give the Aviation a test flight. Once you nail it down, you can regale your guests with tales of your experimental mixology, like a mad scientist who, instead of creating a monster, created something delicious!

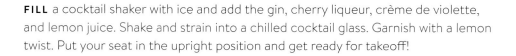

FILL a cocktail shaker with ice and add the gin, cherry liqueur, crème de violette, and lemon juice. Shake and strain into a chilled cocktail glass. Garnish with a lemon twist. Put your seat in the upright position and get ready for takeoff!

COCKTAIL #56—LONDON CALLING

The song—"I'm Your Boogie Man" by KC and the Sunshine Band

Ice

1¾ ounces gin

½ ounce fresh lemon juice

¼ ounce simple syrup (page 112)

½ ounce dry Spanish sherry

3 dashes of orange bitters

Tipsy and I absolutely love London and all things British. My mom's side of the family was British, so it's in my blood. On my first trip outside of the United States when I was thirteen, I went to London and became obsessed with the idea that I was standing on a different continent. I kept marveling that there was a whole ocean between Michigan and me.

During that trip, Elvis Presley died. It's very strange to be in a foreign land when an American institution passes away. I remember that the only thing the British press seemed to talk about was how Elvis never played in the UK. I also remember thinking that Elvis had really missed out.

London is always calling out to Tipsy and me, which is why when I first saw the name of this drink, I knew I had to make it. I love all the ingredients and was intrigued by the idea of adding sherry to a cocktail. There was a running joke on a great British TV show called *The Royle Family* in which the grandmother always says she never drinks except for a small glass of sherry each night, then gets plowed on all other manner of booze. So the presence of sherry in this drink seemed like the perfect nod to faux temperance. And it turns out that it works with the other ingredients wonderfully. This is simply a very good drink.

London is calling. Will you accept the charges?

FILL a cocktail shaker with ice and add the rest of the ingredients. Shake and strain into a chilled cocktail glass. Get it down your throat! (Emilia Clarke taught me that pub toast. Yes, I am a name-dropper.)

COCKTAIL #57—GREYHOUND/ SALTY DOG

The song—"Who Let the Dogs Out" by Baha Men

We love Scottish Terriers. Our current Scottie, Buster, puts up with a lot. He's been on my cocktail show several times, usually in some sort of ridiculous outfit, like a Batman or UPS delivery costume. He doesn't love it, but he goes with it. Tipsy and I have been together so long that we've had several Scotties. There were Dean Martin, Dylan, Linus, and Mary before Buster came along.

When you're into Scotties, people like to buy you Scottie gifts. Turns out there are lots of things in this world with Scotties printed on them. One of the gifts we receive the most is artwork from Black & White Scotch Whisky ads from the 1940s and '50s. They all feature a Scottie and a West Highland White Terrier who are friends. They still make Black & White Scotch, and the two dogs are still on the label.

So we must be talking about a drink that features scotch, right? Wrong! This one uses either gin or vodka. But both these drinks are named after dogs. And there you go. Feig logic.

These two drinks are made from the same ingredients with one small difference—salt. So if you like booze and grapefruit juice and occasionally crave sodium, you're barking up the right trees here! (More puns! Dad humor! And I'm not even a dad. Well, except to my dog.)

GREYHOUND

Ice

1½ ounces gin or vodka

Fresh grapefruit juice

Lime wheel

FILL a highball glass with ice, add the gin or vodka, fill the rest with grapefruit juice, and stir. Garnish with a lime wheel and wolf it down!

SALTY DOG

Sea salt or coarse kosher salt

Ice

1½ ounces gin or vodka

3 ounces fresh grapefruit juice

WET the lip of a highball glass and dip the rim in a plate of salt, then fill it with ice. Place more ice in a cocktail shaker and add the gin or vodka and grapefruit juice. Shake and strain into the glass. Hot dog!

COCKTAIL #58—BLUSHING BRIDE

The song—"Hold On" by Wilson Phillips

As you may or may not know, I directed a movie called *Bridesmaids*. When I first took the job, I had a lot of trepidation because, truth be told, I didn't like weddings. Ever since I was a kid, I hated how weddings I went to were run. The ceremony was always too long; it took forever for the reception to get started as you waited for the photographer to take all the photos of the wedding party; once the reception started, it took even longer for the food to come out; and the wedding cake you'd been staring at for hours wouldn't be cut and served until the end of the evening. They may have made the bride and groom happy, but as parties they were simply not much fun.

When Tipsy and I decided to get married, we wanted to avoid all these issues. We got married in Las Vegas in a big event hall at the Treasure Island Hotel with more than a hundred friends and family and sat everybody at the tables they'd be eating at. We had a five-minute-long ceremony, and as soon as we were pronounced husband and wife, we announced that dinner was served and revealed a huge, ready-to-go buffet. We'd placed a small wedding cake on each table and told everybody they could cut the cake whenever they wanted as long as someone took a picture of them doing it. Then we partied all night with an Elvis impersonator and a live band. People still tell us more than twenty-five years later that it was the most fun wedding they had ever been to.

I've been to some pretty great weddings since then, as well as some more ordinary ones. But at the time, the thought of immersing myself in a wedding movie and spending a year of my life thinking about weddings seemed like an imperfect fit. However, I ended up having the time of my life directing the film with that wonderful cast, and people still seem to like watching it to this day.

In honor of that, here are two variations on a wedding-themed drink that feature Champagne or sparkling wine. Because you can't have a wedding without bubbles!

BLUSHING BRIDE #1

1 ounce peach schnapps

1 ounce grenadine

4 ounces chilled Champagne or sparkling wine

POUR the schnapps and grenadine into a Champagne flute, then top with the Champagne. Stir gently to combine. You'll definitely say "I do!"

BLUSHING BRIDE #2

2 ounces chilled St. Germain elderflower liqueur

4 ounces chilled Champagne or sparkling wine

½ ounce grenadine

PUT the St. Germain in a Champagne flute, then top with Champagne. Pour in the grenadine to add the blush. Stir gently to combine. Drink now or forever hold your peace!

COCKTAIL #59—ADIOS, MOTHERFUCKER!

The song—"Wonderful Night" by Fatboy Slim

Ice

½ ounce vodka

½ ounce light rum

½ ounce white tequila

½ ounce gin

½ ounce blue Curaçao

2 ounces sweet-and-sour mix (see Note)

Sprite or 7-Up (or club soda if you want less sugar)

Lemon wedge or wheel

Cocktail cherry

Some drinks are just evil. This is one of them. It has an evil name, like a catchphrase from an '80s cop film. It's filled with liquors that aren't evil on their own but become incredibly evil when combined. My friend Bruce McCulloch of *Kids in the Hall* fame has a name for drinks like this: "shit mixes." Well, this drink is indeed a shit mix.

So why am I telling you how to make it? Well, believe it or not, it's really, really good. It's an incredibly tasty drink that goes down wonderfully smooth. *That's* why it's so evil. But, hey, what's life without a little bit of evil in it from time to time? Good luck!

FILL a highball or Tom Collins glass with ice and add the vodka, rum, tequila, gin, Curaçao, and sweet-and-sour mix. Stir and top with soda. Garnish with a lemon wedge or wheel and a cherry. *Adios!*

NOTE: To make your own sweet-and-sour mix, combine one part water with one part sugar and add lime juice to taste. No need to heat it up.

COCKTAIL #60—THE ALGONQUIN COCKTAIL

The song—"Super Freak" by Rick James

Ice

1½ ounces rye whiskey

¾ ounce dry vermouth

¾ ounce pineapple juice

I've always been a fan of the Algonquin Round Table, a group of writers and humorists who met for lunch at the Algonquin Hotel in New York City on weekdays from 1919 until 1929. Famous for their biting wit and intellect, they were the writer Dorothy Parker; *New Yorker* cofounder Harold Ross; columnists Robert Benchley, Franklin Pierce Adams, and Heywood Broun; Broun's wife, Ruth Hale; the critic Alexander Woollcott; the great Harpo Marx; and the playwrights George S. Kaufman, Marc Connelly, Edna Ferber, and Robert E. Sherwood.

When I was a standup comedian in Los Angeles in the 1980s, I was lucky enough to join my own round table. My friends and fellow comedy performers Steve and Dave Higgins lived in a run-down house in the Valley that we called "The Ranch." A bunch of us would gather there after our comedy club gigs to sit around a table playing poker and make one another laugh until the sun came up. It was truly one of the most fun times of my life. This went on for about four years, until Steve and Dave and our friend Dave "Gruber" Allen got a show called *The Higgins Boys and Gruber* on the new Comedy Channel. They got rid of the house and moved to New York City, and the rest of us headed off to pursue our own careers in comedy.

That fun of close camaraderie with a group of very like-minded people with whom we can laugh and learn is something we should all get to experience at some point.

So, in honor of the Algonquin Round Table and the Ranch Round Table and any other group of fun and funny friends sitting in a circle having the time of their lives, I give you the Algonquin Cocktail!

FILL a cocktail shaker with ice and add the rye, vermouth, and pineapple juice. Shake and strain into a chilled cocktail glass. Have a ball!

COCKTAIL #61—GEORGIA MINT JULEP

The song—"Mint Car" by the Cure

Is anyone else out there a contrarian? Do you like to throw in an opposing viewpoint just to stir up conversation—or trouble? Do you see the one way to do something, the way everybody else likes and is used to, and say, "Let's do it a different way"? Do people like you for it? Or do they think you're a big pain in the ass? Well, they might be annoyed with you, but you know what? They'll often learn something from the unexpected way you do something. And whether they'll admit it or not, they'll be grateful to you for opening their minds and expanding their horizons. *Or* they'll never want to hang out with you again.

Either way, life is more interesting when you try the unexpected. So, sure, I could tell you how to make a mint julep. They're delicious and a total crowd-pleaser. I drank a bunch of authentic mint juleps many years ago at a party in Kentucky for the Derby with other cast members from the movie *Ski Patrol*, of which I was one of the stars. The party was thrown by a rich horse-owning family; they put a free pack of cigarettes on each dinner plate as a welcome gift and positioned wrestlers in cages around the ballroom, and everybody got roaring drunk in their tuxedoes and beautiful gowns. It was like being in a Fellini movie. The night ended when I was waiting for a car to pick me up and saw a glamorous woman barf down the front of her very expensive dress. So when I tell you I've been around mint juleps, you can take my word for it.

But you could find a mint julep recipe anywhere. I'm here to be your boozy contrarian! If someone asks for a mint julep, you can surprise them with this Georgia Mint Julep instead. What's the difference? Instead of bourbon, it uses Cognac and peach brandy. Georgia peaches? Get it? Georgia mint julep? Good! So get some mint, grab your muddler, and set to work making this delicious, contrary julep!

Several fresh mint leaves, plus a mint sprig for garnish

1 teaspoon sugar

Dash of water

2 ounces Cognac

1 ounce peach brandy

Crushed ice

MUDDLE several mint leaves with the sugar and water in an old fashioned glass or specialized julep cup. Add the Cognac and brandy. Fill with crushed ice and stir vigorously. Insert a mint sprig at the side of the glass for garnish. Giddyup!

COCKTAIL #62—NAPOLEON

The song—"Rock Steady" by Aretha Franklin

Ice

2 ounces gin

½ ounce orange liqueur (Cointreau, Grand Marnier, or other)

½ ounce Dubonnet Rouge apéritif

I was a Bugs Bunny fanatic as a kid. My friend Dave Fleury and I would sit at the lunch table in the cafeteria and recite by heart the dialogue from entire Bugs Bunny cartoons. We'd laugh our heads off and everybody would watch us from other tables like we were the biggest weirdos in the school. But we had the greatest time every day. Some days, when my bullies were extra-aggressive, it was the only thing that got me through my morning classes, knowing that Dave and I were going to have the time of our lives as soon as the lunch bell rang.

There was one Bugs Bunny cartoon in which Bugs runs up against Napoleon and keeps calling him "Nappy." Dave and I just thought that was hilarious. Whenever our history teacher would talk about Napoleon, Dave and I couldn't look at each other and had to stifle our laughter because all we wanted to do was blurt out "Nappy" at the teacher.

Did I mention that Dave and I were nerds? We didn't wear glasses and snort when we laughed, or wear flood pants and have pocket pencil protectors in our short-sleeved shirts. No, we were real nerds, not the cartoon version you used to see on TV all the time. We were just a couple of awkward guys who knew what we liked and enjoyed it with each other. And that to me is the very definition of being a nerd. Or, as we're called now, geeks. (If you're a *Freaks and Geeks* fan, in the pilot episode I originally had the geeks reciting lines from Bugs Bunny cartoons to one another, but we eventually changed it to lines from *Caddyshack* because Judd Apatow worried that Looney Tunes dialogue was perhaps *too* geeky. He was probably right.)

This is all a long way of letting you know why I first stopped on the recipe for the Napoleon cocktail when I came across it in my *Mr. Boston* book. I laughed and said "Nappy" to myself, then looked closer and saw that it was made with three of my favorite ingredients. So you have Bugs Bunny to thank for this truly delicious drink, which Tipsy refers to as one of her "top ten." Geek it up!

FILL a cocktail shaker with ice and add the rest of the ingredients. Shake and strain into a chilled cocktail glass. Nappy time!

COCKTAIL #63—JAPANESE SLIPPER

(OR, WHAT SHOULD HAVE BEEN THE *GHOSTBUSTERS* COCKTAIL)

The song—"Favourite Shirts (Boy Meets Girl)" by Haircut 100

Ice

1 ounce Midori
melon liqueur

1 ounce Cointreau
orange liqueur

1 ounce fresh
lemon juice

Cocktail cherry

Okay, when I made a cocktail in honor of my film *Ghostbusters: Answer the Call* on my cocktail show (page 80), I had completely forgotten about Midori. That melon-flavored liqueur is about as green as a liquid can get without being antifreeze and is the perfect visual substitute for ectoplasmic slime. And yet, the drink I made in honor of my movie used green Chartreuse, which only made the cocktail slightly yellow. So, basically, I blew it.

When I made *Ghostbusters*, we spent a lot of time trying to get the formula for our ectoplasm right. It all came down to color and viscosity. Simply put, the ooze needed to be green enough to pop visually and thick enough to slowly drip down without being so viscous that it moved like a slug. After paring all our options down to several microvariations of the formula and doing lots of comparison tests, we eventually decided on the ideal mix that both sprayed and flowed perfectly. And it was really, really green.

Well, so is this drink! It's a fun mix of fruity flavors that combine to taste a lot like a SweeTARTS while not being overly sweet. I know that's a pretty dicey description, but it's a really good drink if you don't mind a little tartness. So slip into a Japanese Slipper and see what you think!

FILL a cocktail shaker with ice and add the Midori, Cointreau, and lemon juice. Shake and strain into a chilled cocktail glass. Garnish with a cherry. Green never tasted so good!

COCKTAIL #64—WHITE LADY

The song—"I've Got the Music in Me" by the Kiki Dee Band

Ice

1½ ounces gin

¾ ounce Cointreau
orange liqueur

¾ ounce fresh
lemon juice

½ egg white
(optional)

When I was a teenager, I discovered Steve Martin before anybody else I knew. I got a hold of an early copy of his first comedy album, *Let's Get Small*, and thought it was one of the funniest things I'd ever heard. I used to listen to it in my room every night. I even bought a microphone at RadioShack and a white three-piece suit like Steve's so every evening I could dress up in my room and pretend to be him as I pantomimed his act along with the record.

This would have been weird on its own, but then I decided to start doing his routines for my friends at school. The thing was that nobody had heard the album yet or even knew who Steve Martin was, so they all thought I had made up these routines myself. I started getting fans and would entertain anybody who came by our lunch table by doing Steve's act.

Did I tell anybody that I was doing somebody else's comedy routines? Of course not. I was so happy to be getting big laughs and kudos for being so smart and funny that I just kept it to myself.

But then Steve Martin got famous and his record became a bestseller and very quickly everybody knew I had stolen his act. I immediately went from hero to thief and became the Milli Vanilli of Chippewa Valley High School. And I learned a valuable lesson about plagiarism. That lesson? Don't do it! What *else* could the lesson be?

The cocktail world is sometimes like me with my Steve Martin album—there's a lot of copying that goes on. A mixologist will take a drink, change an ingredient or even the amount of one of the ingredients, call it a different name, and say it's original. I've done it myself. In the cocktail world, even a small variation *does* make a different drink.

Take the White Lady, for example. It's only one ingredient different from the previous drink, the Japanese Slipper. Swap out the Midori in a Japanese Slipper for gin and you've got a White Lady. They're both also pretty close to a Tom Collins and a gimlet and many other drinks that involve a liquor, a liqueur, and some citrus.

One variation to a White Lady that many bartenders like is adding an egg white to it. We've already talked about the pros and cons of using raw egg whites in drinks (see page 91), so all I can tell you is that the White Lady works great with or without it. It's a refreshing and friendly drink that goes down smooth and makes you happy. Just like an old Steve Martin album!

FILL a cocktail shaker with ice and add the rest of the ingredients. Shake (if using an egg white, shake vigorously for at least 30 seconds) and strain into a chilled cocktail glass. It's a wild and crazy drink!

COCKTAIL #65—LEATHERNECK COCKTAIL

The song—"Money" by Ivy Levan

Ice

2 ounces blended whiskey

¾ ounce blue Curaçao

½ ounce fresh lime juice

Lime wheel

I've never been what one would describe as tough. I used to cry at the drop of a hat when I was a kid. I always backed down when I was confronted by bullies. I've never been good at sports. I have no coordination and no competitive spirit when it comes to anything athletic. I was always picked last for school teams. In Little League, I would jump out of the way when the ball was pitched to me, and I'd always duck to avoid a fly ball in the outfield. I couldn't even succeed adjacent to rugged things. I failed miserably as the announcer at one of our high school's football games because I couldn't pronounce the last names of all the Polish-American kids on the team.

So I was not a tough kid, nor am I a tough adult. But you know who *is* tough? A Marine. This drink was invented in 1951 by a newspaper columnist and former Marine named Frank Farrell. *Leatherneck* is a nickname for a Marine—a very tough nickname that any tough person would be proud to be called. The only time anybody uses the words *leather* or *neck* in conjunction with my name is to say, "Wow, the skin on the front of his neck really looks like saggy, thin old leather." (And it does. Ah, aging!)

This drink is tough at its core because its main ingredient is whiskey. And what's a tougher drink than that? So toughen up and make yourself a Leatherneck right now! That's an order!

FILL a cocktail shaker with ice and add the whiskey, Curaçao, and lime juice. Shake and strain into chilled cocktail glass. Garnish with a lime wheel. *Semper fi!*

COCKTAIL #66—HANKY-PANKY

The song—"Play That Funky Music" by Wild Cherry

Ice

1½ ounces gin

1½ ounces sweet vermouth

2 dashes of Fernet-Branca amaro

Orange twist

I was a magician when I was a kid and would do my act in nursing homes for old people in my hometown. My first magic kit was filled with tiny tricks. I used to stand up in front of my octogenarian audience with the world's smallest dice between my fingers and do an amazing trick in which I would change the dots on the dice as I turned them back and forth. Not even a sniper with an ultra-high-powered scope could have seen the microscopic marks on the dice from where they were sitting, but the kind old people smiled and clapped whenever I turned the dice and told them that the values had changed.

Whenever you bought a magic trick, it would come with a sheet of paper with what was called "patter" printed on it, which were the sort of things you could say as you performed the trick. It was always super-inane dialogue along the lines of "And now, ladies and gentlemen, if you'll just look at the end of the tube, I'll produce a string of brightly colored silks" and the occasional joke, usually something like, "Will someone call out any number between sixteen and sixty? Thank you. I only wanted to find out if anyone was still awake." But they always had you say the magic words at some point, which would either be *abracadabra* or *hocus-pocus*.

Well, some linguists say that the term *hanky-panky* originated from *hocus-pocus*. It started out meaning *mischief* and later took on a more sexual connotation. And it found its way to this drink, which is one that people either like or hate. It's the bitter amaro liqueur Fernet-Branca that makes it divisive, with its slightly medicinal taste. So when you first make this drink, go easy on the Fernet-Branca to see how much you can take. You can use the bartenders' trick of putting a straw in the mixing glass after the drink is stirred, putting your finger on the top of the straw to trap the liquid and then removing your finger when you put the straw in your mouth to let the taste hit your tongue to see if you like the mix. If you get the mix where you want it, this can be a really fantastic cocktail.

So work some hocus-pocus on your Hanky-Panky, and abracadabra! You may have a new favorite drink!

FILL a mixing glass with ice and add the gin, sweet vermouth, and Fernet-Branca. Stir well and strain into a chilled cocktail glass. Squeeze an orange twist over the surface of the drink, then drop the twist into the glass. It's magic!

COCKTAIL #67—THE DERBY

The song—"Mask, Gloves, Soap, Scrubs" by Todrick Hall

Ice

1 ounce bourbon

½ ounce sweet vermouth

½ ounce orange Curaçao

¼ ounce fresh lime juice

Fresh mint leaf

Since we didn't use bourbon in our Georgia Mint Julep (page 177) and since this drink has even more of a horse race theme to it, let's make this our official cocktail for the running of the ponies! I used to go to the horse races all the time when I was in my early twenties, not because I liked horse racing but because I loved the world of old-timey horse racing gamblers—guys who chomped cigars and wore checkered jackets and who angrily ripped up their losing bet tickets and threw the pieces on the ground. It all had this great Dashiell Hammett–Damon Runyon–*Guys and Dolls* vibe that seemed really funny to me.

Once I took a few friends of mine to the track and we tried betting on some horses. I only ever picked horses by their names and the color of their jockey's shirt, since trying to handicap from the racing guides was far more work than I was willing to do. Besides, because there are so many variables involved in why a horse will win, picking the most fun name and the prettiest colors seemed about as accurate as looking at all the other, more scientific factors. My friends and I decided on a horse named Telephone Canyon who had huge odds against it, and we each put down twenty bucks.

Well, the race started and Telephone Canyon was immediately in last place. But as the race went on, he slowly worked his way to the front of the bunch and ended up winning by a nose. The whole place was screaming and cheering. My friends and I hugged and jumped up and down and strutted over to the cashier's window chanting "Telephone Canyon! Telephone Canyon!" to collect the fortune we knew we had just made from the huge odds.

We handed our tickets proudly back to the cashier and he handed us each . . . twenty-four dollars. It turns out we only bet on the horse to show, which means we thought it would come in third. The people who bet on it to come in first place won a fortune. Our enthusiasm killed, we slunk away with our four dollars in profits and never went back to the track again.

And with that sad story, please enjoy this truly delicious drink that always comes in first!

FILL a cocktail shaker with ice and add the bourbon, vermouth, Curaçao, and lime juice. Shake and strain into a chilled cocktail glass. Garnish with a mint leaf. Jackpot!

COCKTAIL #68—THE LAST WORD

The song—"Timebomb" by Beck

Do you have a friend or family member who is too much? Someone you like but with whom you have to really weigh whether their presence around other people will cause problems or simply be *too much*? I had a friend in high school who was really funny and very amusing to hang out with one on one. But if I went out in public with him, he would inevitably blurt out the most inappropriate comment about the most dangerous person within earshot.

We were standing in a Burger King once, and some big biker dude in a Hawaiian shirt walked in. My friend said loudly, "God, look at that guy's shirt. It looks like a woman's blouse." My stomach dropped as I watched the biker turn in slow motion and look directly at me, thinking I had said it. He stalked toward me, saying the words that strike terror into any bullied nerd's heart: "You got a problem, pal?"

Desperate to let the guy know that it wasn't me but also not wanting to indict my friend and cause a fight, I lamely blurted out, "We were just reciting lines from a movie."

"What movie?" he asked, clearly not believing me.

Panicking, I squeaked out, "A Bugs Bunny cartoon."

He stared at me blankly for what felt like a year, then snorted and turned away to order his food. I saw my friend getting ready to say something and hissed under my breath, "You say one more word and I'll kill you."

To which he just laughed and said, "You're hilarious, Feig."

If this drink were that Burger King, my friend would have been the green Chartreuse. As we established back in the Bijou Cocktail (page 80), our boozy green pal can very quickly overpower a drink. When I first made this for Tipsy, she didn't like it, even though it's the kind of drink she would normally like. When I suggested that maybe the green Chartreuse was throwing her, she said I may have underpoured the lime juice. Sure enough, when I added a bit more, she liked the

drink much better. She was right—I had put in too little juice. So make sure you really stick to the exact measurements for this one, and adjust by adding a bit more lime juice if it is too Chartreuse-heavy for you.

One last thing: Almost all the recipes for this drink say it should be served straight up in a chilled cocktail glass. I've chosen to suggest you serve it on the rocks in an old fashioned glass. You can do it either way, but I feel like the addition of the ice helps to tame this one a bit more as you drink it. But give it a try either way and see what you and your guests think.

Because when it comes to this drink, you should always have the last word. Clever? Yes. Well, maybe.

Ice

¾ ounce gin

¾ ounce green Chartreuse herbal liqueur

¾ ounce maraschino cherry liqueur

¾ ounce fresh lime juice

FILL a cocktail shaker with ice and add the gin, Chartreuse, cherry liqueur, and lime juice. Shake and strain into an old fashioned glass filled with fresh ice. Word up!

COCKTAIL #69—THE AMBER ROOM

The song—"Livin' in America" by James Brown

Ice

¾ ounce gin

¾ ounce Noilly Prat Ambré vermouth

¼ ounce St. Germain elderflower liqueur

2 dashes of orange bitters

Lemon twist

Tipsy and I took a one-week barge trip down the Canal du Midi in the South of France a couple of times in the 2000s (yes, this was the same barge from page 77 when it rained the whole week). The barge started in a tiny town called Homps, slowly made its way down the canal, and ended its journey in Marseillan, a small fishing village on the banks of a lake. There I discovered one of my favorite vermouths, Noilly Prat. We took a tour of the distillery and the shop where you could buy bottles of their usually white and red vermouths. There we also tried a viscous, amber-colored, absolutely delicious vermouth called Noilly Prat Ambré. Infused with thirteen herbs and spices, it was frankly one of the best apéritifs I've ever had.

The problem is it's not sold in the United States. We've run across a rogue bottle or two in liquor stores here but mostly we live off those we've smuggled back in our suitcases and ration it out for only the most special of occasions.

So why am I giving you a recipe if you're going to have trouble sourcing an ingredient? Well, I firmly believe that if something is great, it will eventually get out into the world. The optimist in me believes that Noilly Prat can't keep this wonderful spirit away from us forever. When you eventually get your hands on a bottle, have a few glasses straight up to appreciate all it has to offer, then make this fantastic drink!

FILL a mixing glass with ice and add the gin, Noilly Prat Ambré, St. Germain, and bitters. Stir well until very cold, then strain into a chilled cocktail glass. Garnish with a lemon twist. Get trapped in this amber!

COCKTAIL #70—BATIDA ROSA

The song—"Oiseau Fâché" by Thomas Dutronc

As poor Tipsy Faunt can tell you, I have a bit of an obsessive personality. Once I decide to start collecting things, I can't stop. I can turn any fun hobby into an upsetting, compulsive quest to obtain anything and everything related to it. This has manifested itself at various points in my life into collections of:

- PEZ dispensers
- Snow globes
- Wristwatches
- Mechanical pencils
- Pocket watches
- Suits
- Ties
- Pocket silks
- Lapel flowers
- Briefcases
- Cuff links
- LEGO kits
- Cocktail glasses
- Fezzes
- Shoes

Ice

2 ounces cachaça

1 ounce pineapple juice

½ ounce fresh lemon juice

½ ounce grenadine

1 ounce club soda

Orange wheel

And booze. The second I read a cocktail recipe that has any ingredient I don't have, even if it's incredibly obscure, I have to get a bottle of it. It's why my home bar looks like a bottle hoarder's. But in my defense, I just want to be able to make any cocktail I come across. I want to be able to invent drinks that no one has ever thought of before. I want to be the King of Cocktails!

Well, okay, not really the king. Just someone who can make anything. And that's the reason I have a couple of bottles of cachaça, a distilled spirit made from fermented sugarcane juice and the most popular alcohol in Brazil. It's very close to rum, and yet completely different at the same time. To be perfectly honest, the first time you open the bottle and smell it, you may wince a bit. It really doesn't smell very good. But once you put it into a cocktail, it really works.

The most famous drink that uses cachaça is a caipirinha, which is just cachaça with muddled limes and sugar over ice. It's an incredibly good drink that goes down disturbingly smooth. I always thought that was the best use of cachaça until I came across this recipe. It's just a little more fun and flavorful and doesn't pack quite the punch of a caipirinha, which makes it the perfect drink for a hot summer day.

So get yourself a bottle of cachaça, don't smell it when you open it, and make this delicious sparkling cooler!

FILL a cocktail shaker with ice and add the cachaça, juices, and grenadine. Shake and strain into a wineglass filled with fresh ice. Top with club soda and garnish with an orange wheel. *Saúde!*

COCKTAIL #71—WEEP-NO-MORE COCKTAIL

The song—"Right Action" by Franz Ferdinand

Ice

¾ ounce Dubonnet Rouge apéritif

¾ ounce brandy

¼ teaspoon maraschino cherry liqueur

Juice of half a lime

If you read the story accompanying the Leatherneck Cocktail (page 184), you already know I cried a lot as a kid. It's too bad I didn't have this drink as an elixir back then. (Not that my parents would have let me booze it up back then; I was annoying but not that annoying.) On paper, this cocktail doesn't sound like it will work. There are four very different tastes dogpiling into your shaker (hello, Hot Pants!), ready to fight it out for the win like a group of desperate actors all auditioning for the same role.

But somehow it all works, and it works incredibly well. The lime brings the other three disparate tastes together, creating a smooth drink that also looks quite beautiful. Even Tipsy had to give it up for this one, and she was horrified when she heard the ingredients going into it.

Don't take our word for it—see for yourself. You won't be weeping over this one, unless delicious drinks move you to tears!

FILL a cocktail shaker with ice and add the rest of the ingredients. Shake and strain into a chilled cocktail glass. Cheer up!

COCKTAIL #72—PINK PEARL COCKTAIL

The song—"Timebomb" by Kylie Minogue

Ice

1½ ounces gin

1 ounce Giffard Crème de Pamplemousse Rose grapefruit liqueur

½ ounce Aperol aperitivo

1 ounce fresh grapefruit juice

3 to 4 ounces prosecco

I'm gonna brag. Tipsy and I are friends with Kylie Minogue. That's right, I just name-dropped. Wouldn't you if you were friends with Kylie? Tipsy was getting her hair done in Paris years ago, and Kylie was sitting in the chair next to her. They started talking, and next thing we knew, she and three very fun and interesting friends of hers were joining us for an impromptu party in our hotel that very evening! Yes, sometimes very cool things happen to me. I like to think it's the universe making up for all the bullies I had to put up with as a kid.

Kylie has remained a close friend of ours, and so, for her birthday, I wanted to honor her on my cocktail show. We asked her if she had a drink she wanted us to make and she suggested one of her favorites, the Pink Pearl. Guess what? Now it's one of Tipsy's and my favorites, too! It's a sneaky little drink because it's got a lot of booze in it and packs a not-so-secret punch. On top of that, it tastes a bit like ice cream. How can you go wrong?

So mix yourself up a Pink Pearl and raise your glass to the great Kylie Minogue before you enjoy it. And, of course, make sure you put on her music so you can dance the night away as you sip!

FILL a cocktail shaker with ice and add the gin, Crème de Pamplemousse Rose, Aperol, and grapefruit juice. Shake and strain into a chilled Champagne flute or white wine glass. Top with the prosecco. Cheers, lovers!

COCKTAIL #73—FINE-AND-DANDY

The song—"Safe and Sound" by Capital Cities

Ice

1½ ounces gin

½ ounce Cointreau orange liqueur or triple sec

Juice of ¼ lemon

Dash of bitters

Cocktail cherry

I've always been an optimist. Or at least I've always tried to be one. When I was a kid, I would wake up each morning feeling happy and ready for all the great things I knew would happen to me that day. And then school and bullies and all the obstacles and judgments and failures that came at me would grind me down, so by the end of the day, I would drag my tired and demoralized formerly optimistic self to bed and fall onto my mattress feeling like the world was a much tougher place than I wanted it to be. But then the next morning I would wake up just as optimistic, ready once again to blindly take on the slings and arrows of the day, certain that I would succeed and make it through better than the previous one. Sadly, the day usually kicked my ass once again. But I never stopped being an optimist because of my unwavering view that the world would eventually not let me down if I worked hard enough and kept my positive attitude. And over the years, enough good things have happened for me that I will always believe keeping an optimistic view of the world and the people in it is the way to go.

In other words, as far as I'm concerned, rose-colored glasses are better than dirty ones.

When I came across a drink with a name that reflected how I think life should always feel for every person on this planet, I was intrigued. To me, the phrase "fine and dandy" means that not only are things going well; you're also in a good, optimistic mood. Obviously life can't always be like that, but it's the state of mind we can strive for, both for ourselves and for everybody else in this world.

So mix yourself up one of these as a reminder to always strive for the fine-and-dandy in life. It almost tastes like lemonade, and what's more positive than a glass of lemonade? Here's to making lemonade out of all the lemons that life hands us!

FILL a cocktail shaker with ice and add the gin, Cointreau, lemon juice, and bitters. Shake and strain into a chilled cocktail glass. Garnish by dropping in the cherry. You'll be fine!

COCKTAIL #74—STANLEY COCKTAIL

The song—"Get Outta My Dreams, Get into My Car" by Billy Ocean

Ice

¾ ounce gin

¼ ounce light rum

1 teaspoon grenadine

Juice of ¼ lemon

Yes, I was in a movie called *Ski Patrol* that came out in 1990. It bombed at the box office, but once it started playing on cable, it was apparently watched by every kid who grew up in the '90s. It's not a great movie, but over the years I would get recognized by young folks who knew it by heart because they had seen it tens of times. It's one of the reasons I love movies and TV. Once something exists, even if gets bad reviews when it comes out (and *Ski Patrol* definitely got bad reviews), it can eventually find its audience and rehabilitate itself. Hooray for recorded media!

In the film, I played a character called Stanley, a janitor whose dream it was to join the brave men and women of the ski patrol. Of course, there was a ski lodge run by a kindly older man that an evil land developer wanted to buy and tear down, which was pretty much the story in every 1980s and '90s comedy. In the business, we called it the "snobs-versus-slobs" genre. The classic snobs-versus-slobs movie is *Animal House*, a truly funny (although definitely not-PC) film, which then spawned many substandard copies. But this tried-and-true formula allowed funny people to run amok and take revenge on mean rich people.

My character was originally supposed to be a guy who had . . . ahem . . . uncontrollable erections. Yes, whenever the pretty girl I liked would talk to me, I was supposed to have to duck down behind a couch or chair to hide my indelicate condition. Fortunately, they decided before production to make the movie more kid-friendly, so I was spared the indignity of portraying the bearer of uncontrollable boners on the big screen. But I did get to do not one but *two* dance numbers in the movie, both of which I completely underwhelmed in. But it was a fun movie to make and I made some great friends doing it.

It was only natural that when I ran across a drink called the Stanley Cocktail, I had to make it. And the happy irony is that it's really good. It's not a well-known drink at all, so when I found it, I felt a bit like a boozy archaeologist who had unearthed a beautiful clay pot from some ancient civilization. So mix one up and raise a toast to your favorite in-control-of-his-boners ski patrol member!

FILL a cocktail shaker with ice and add the rest of the ingredients. Shake and strain into a chilled cocktail glass. It's a good stiff drink! (I'm truly sorry for that boner groaner.)

COCKTAIL #75—LOVE POTION

The song—"Together Forever" by Rick Astley

Ice

3 ounces gin

1 ounce fresh lime juice

1 ounce St. Germain elderflower liqueur

Up to 6 ounces chilled rosé Champagne or sparkling rosé wine

MAKES 2 COCKTAILS

Love! Who doesn't love *love*? I spent the first twenty-seven years of my life desperately searching for love. I remember wishing that whatever cosmic being is in charge of everything would just come down and pair us all up with our perfect mates so that we could stop the often painful and futile-feeling quest for the love of our life.

I had totally hit the rocks when it came to love back then. I'd had a couple of failed relationships, both with fellow performers who were great people but with whom I ultimately didn't mesh. I had then pursued a couple of women I thought I was in love with who had zero interest in me as a paramour. After the second of these quests blew up in my face, I declared that I was officially giving up on love. I would lead the life of a bachelor, although not a playboy. I would throw myself into my career and have great friends and try to be fabulous and forget about finding my perfect partner.

And, of course, the minute I stopped being so desperate, I met my future wife. I actually met Laurie, aka Tipsy Faunt, in a professional capacity. After I finished filming my role in the movie *Ski Patrol*, my managers fired me. I was in shock, since I figured that being one of the stars of a major motion picture would mean I was now a top client. Sadly, they didn't consider *Ski Patrol* to be a major motion picture. They considered it to be a joke. So I suddenly found myself with no real representation in a town where you definitely need someone advocating for you.

I told my costar in the film, former VH1 veejay Roger Rose, that I needed a new manager, and he told me about a friend of his, a woman named Laurie Gilbert. I had a meeting with her and realized we'd met a couple of times before at parties over the past year. One was a goodbye party at the Ranch (see page 176), because my friends were moving to NYC to star on their own Comedy Channel show and our time in our comedy clubhouse was ending. Laurie had shown up with her sister, Peggy, but my friends and I were all so sad about the Ranch that we didn't pay much attention to them (but I did secretly think Laurie was cute, even though I had no idea who she was).

The second time we had met was at my friend Wayne Federman's apartment watching the Cubs play in the World Series. I showed up and when Laurie saw me, she ran over and literally jumped on me, hugging me tightly. She'd just seen a short film I'd starred in and thought I was really good in it. But beyond that very friendly greeting, we didn't really talk—although I did notice that she laughed at all my jokes (the ultimate aphrodisiac for a comedy person), and I still thought she was incredibly cute.

So I went to meet this new potential manager and was very surprised to find it was that same woman. We talked for an hour, hit it off, and decided to work together. We were client and manager for two weeks, and then romance blossomed. We dated for four years. I knew she was the one, but I was too afraid to commit. But then one night in 1994, at 4:30 a.m., our house was rocked by a major earthquake. It was the infamous Northridge earthquake, which caused widespread damage across Los Angeles. It was such a terrifying event that I remember thinking I needed to grow up and commit to this wonderful person whom I had just been through a life-and-death experience with.

So I proposed and we got married. As of this writing, we just celebrated our twenty-ninth wedding anniversary. Laurie was my love potion, and that potion has never worn off. I've loved her with all my heart from the very beginning of our more than thirty years together, and I love her more and more each day.

For those of you still searching for The One, all I can say is try to relax. Don't be desperate. Just keep your heart and your mind open to the people you meet. You'll find your love potion—I guarantee it. But until you do, here's one (that serves two!) you can make at home today! Get ready to fall in love!

FILL two wineglasses with ice, then put the gin, lime juice, and St. Germain into a cocktail shaker. Add ice, then shake and strain equal amounts into the wineglasses. Top with the Champagne. (Be careful to not put in more Champagne than the recipe calls for. Too much will dilute the taste. Start with less than 3 ounces per glass, then take a sip and add more if needed.) Heart this drink!

COCKTAIL #76—EQUALITY COCKTAIL

ANOTHER PAUL FEIG ORIGINAL

The song—"What I Like About You" by the Romantics

Ice

1 ounce Kahlúa coffee liqueur

1 ounce dark crème de cacao

1 ounce milk or cream

Since I was doing my cocktail show during the Black Lives Matter protests of summer 2020, I wanted to try to create a cocktail that would symbolize how we all feel the world should work. I had great angst about presenting it because I worried it would come off as trite at best and tone-deaf at worst. But my heart was in the right place. I swear.

In short, I wanted to make a cocktail in which black, brown, and white would coexist in perfect harmony. It sounds insanely trite even as I type this. But it's also a really good drink. So do give it a try. If you make it with milk instead of cream, it's not as much of a dessert drink as it is more of a White Russian. I made my original recipe with nonfat Lactaid milk, so you can even enjoy this if you're lactose intolerant.

Anyway, here's to a sane and harmonious future with liberty, justice, and happiness for all!

FILL a rocks glass with ice and add the rest of the ingredients. Stir, sip, and love the world!

COCKTAIL #77—KNICKERBOCKER À LA MONSIEUR

The song—"The Batman Theme" by Neal Hefti and His Orchestra

Crushed ice

2 ounces white or gold rum

½ ounce orange Curaçao

½ ounce raspberry syrup

1 ounce fresh lemon juice

1 orange slice

1 pineapple spear

Yes, we dressed up our dog Buster as Batman for the episode of the show this drink was featured on. What of it? I'm a big fan of cosplay, and why shouldn't that extend to my dog as well? I've been going to Comic-Con for almost thirty years, and while I don't personally dress as my favorite sci-fi characters when I go, I love seeing the creativity people put into their costumes. To me, cosplay represents a confidence in who we are and what we like, and a desire to entertain others by sharing our obsessions openly and creatively. People may make fun of those who do cosplay, but I say to them, who are you to make fun of anyone's self-expression? The people who do cosplay aren't affected by your cynicism. They're having fun and sharing that fun with other like-minded people.

There's way too much judgment in this world about what people should and shouldn't do. If you want to dress up as your favorite movie or comic book character, you should do it. If somebody laughs at you or makes fun of you, that's on them. That's *their* shortcoming. I can almost guarantee they secretly wish they had the nerve to do it themselves, that there's a character or statement they'd love to present to the world and they're too uptight to give in to it. And that's just sad for them. Life's too short to care what other people think, and as long as what you're doing doesn't hurt anyone else, physically or emotionally, then all bets are off.

In short, let your freak flag fly, my friends! When you do, here's a delicious drink that tastes like boozy Jolly Rancher candy. It'll knickerbocker your socks off!

FILL a Tom Collins glass with crushed ice. Add the white or gold rum, Curaçao, raspberry syrup, and lemon juice, and stir. Garnish with the fruit and serve. *Oui oui!*

COCKTAIL #78—GLOOM LIFTER

The song—"Why Can't We Be Friends?" by War

Depression. We all feel it from time to time. Some people have clinical issues with depression that go beyond everyday mood swings and should seek help from professionals so they can lead their best possible lives. But for most of us, depression is something that just comes in the toolbox of being human.

I used to have a lot of problems with depression. Part of it was that I was lonely before I met Laurie and would have times of despair, then look for misguided ways to take control of it. The worst of my misguided ways was gambling.

When I was an actor, I would get a nice paycheck on the rare occasions I got hired on a TV show or movie. And then I would later also get the occasional residual check, which is a small payment for every time they run one of those performances on TV. These checks could be anywhere from a few dollars all the way up to a few thousand dollars, depending on how big the project was.

I had done just enough jobs that sometimes a five-hundred-dollar check would show up in my mailbox. And when I was depressed, the jolt I would get from having one of these checks arrive always convinced me to parlay it into something I thought would cheer me up: going to Vegas.

When a check would arrive in the morning mail, I'd declare to my roommate that we were going to jump in the car after lunch and drive straight through to Las Vegas, about four hours away from Los Angeles. We'd arrive and I'd go immediately to the craps table. I loved playing craps because it was such an exciting game, especially when you were at a "hot table" that gets on a run. The table would be surrounded by people and, when the dice rolled in our favor, the cheers that would burst from the table and the camaraderie it would inspire was intoxicating. I was absolutely hooked on it.

I would invariably double or triple my money on that first table I would visit. The minute I lost, I had the discipline to cash in my chips and get out of there. Once a table went "cold," you knew it. My roommate and I would go and have a big supper with my winnings, and I always knew that we should just get a hotel room, have a fun and relaxing evening, and drive back the next morning.

But . . .

During dinner I'd start to think to myself, *I'm on a roll and we just spent a good amount of my winnings on this meal. If we get a hotel room, that will eat up more of my winnings, so I should play one more round to get my money up even higher so I can still leave Las Vegas with a profit.* Then I'd head to another table, put my money down, and quickly lose it all.

This meant I'd have to drive back from Vegas at about 1:00 a.m. and not get to LA until 5:00 in the morning. The ride back was more depressing than the original depression I was trying to fight by coming to Vegas, and I'd be struggling to not fall asleep at the wheel the entire drive. It was just awful. And yet the next time a residual check showed up, I would do the same thing over again.

Fortunately, I met Laurie. The minute I fell in love, I lost all desire to gamble. To this day, I don't have any urge to do it. I now fight depression by walking, which I read that Charles Dickens used to do when he was beset by depressive feelings. He'd walk from one side of London to the other and figure out what he would write, and so self-medicate in the most natural way possible.

Life is all about lifting gloom and finding joy where you can—hence this drink. It may bring you a bit of joy because it's really delicious. (Obviously, don't ever use alcohol as a cure for depression.) For lack of a better description, the Gloom Lifter tastes a bit like raspberry sherbet, not too sweet and simply quite delightful. It does have egg white in it, which we've discussed the pros and cons of before (see page 91). But I wouldn't advise making this drink without it. The foam on top is all part of the fun, as well as the taste. So break an egg and take on your gloom with this very upbeat drink!

1½ ounces Irish whiskey

½ ounce Cognac

2 teaspoons raspberry syrup

¼ ounce simple syrup (page 112)

1 ounce fresh lemon juice

½ egg white

Ice

COMBINE the whiskey, Cognac, syrups, lemon juice, and egg white in a cocktail shaker and shake without ice for 1 minute to foam it up. Add ice and shake for 1 minute more. Strain into a chilled cocktail glass. Goodbye, gloom!

COCKTAIL #79—FLAMINGO COCKTAIL

The song—"How I Feel" by Flo Rida

Ice

1½ ounces gin

½ ounce apricot brandy

1 teaspoon grenadine

Juice of ½ lime

There are quite a few cocktails with the word *flamingo* in the name. I like this one because it's a little more grown-up than some of the other recipes, which are generally rum-based and have a lot of fruit juice in them. I would dare call this one the most sophisticated cocktails based on an extremely pink bird.

My grandmother lived in Florida for a while when I was a kid, and we used to drive down from Michigan to visit her every winter for our vacation, since my dad owned a store and could only take a vacation during the slow season. It was on one of these trips that I saw my first real live flamingo, as well as thousands of those plastic ones you stick in your lawn. It prompted my lifelong love of all things colorful and fun.

I say never be afraid to bring a lot of color into your life. Even if you're wearing something dark, add something that jumps out color-wise. Because a lot of my suits are dark gray, blue, and brown, I love to put on a fun-colored tie and pocket silk, as well as one of the many colorful silk boutonnières that I've collected over the years. It's a way both to look good and to let the world know that I'm not taking it all too seriously.

So put on a colorful outfit and mix up a couple of Flamingos to complete your look!

FILL a cocktail shaker with ice and add the rest of the ingredients. Shake and strain into a chilled cocktail glass. Think pink!

COCKTAIL #80—TEQUILA SUNRISE

The song—"You Make Me Feel (Mighty Real)" by Sylvester

Ice

1 teaspoon grenadine

1 teaspoon crème de cassis black currant liqueur

1½ ounces tequila

¾ ounce orange Curaçao

½ ounce fresh lime juice

2½ ounces fresh orange juice

I'm in showbiz. I make movies and television shows. My job is to entertain people with the things I do. A lot of the entertainment is in the stories I tell and the actors I use to tell them. But it's also about the way things look and the pageantry with which we do things on screen. Life's too short to not have as much pageantry as possible, I say. In other words, it's always better to put on a show!

There's a boring way to make a delicious drink like the Tequila Sunrise, and then there's a way to put on a show in a glass! At its heart, a Tequila Sunrise is really just tequila, orange juice, and grenadine. That's a fine combo in itself. But if somebody gave you the choice to ride to dinner in the back of a cargo van or in a luxury limousine, wouldn't you pick the limo?

Well, friends, here's the luxury limo version of a Tequila Sunrise, one that takes the standard recipe and makes it more delicious while also adding the visual pageantry that a showbiz professional like me would love to dazzle you with. It's showtime!

FILL a Tom Collins glass with ice and pour in the grenadine and cassis. Fill a cocktail shaker with ice and add the tequila, Curaçao, lime juice, and orange juice. Shake, then strain slowly and carefully into the glass so that the mixture sits on the base of grenadine and cassis, creating a sunrise effect. Take a few seconds to appreciate the visual, then enjoy this wonderful libation. This is one sunrise worth getting up for!

COCKTAIL #81—THE ROYAL SMILE

The song—"Shake It Up" by the Cars

Ice

1 ounce gin

1 ounce Calvados apple brandy

½ ounce fresh lemon juice

¼ ounce simple syrup (page 112)

1 teaspoon grenadine

Lemon twist

One of my dreams in life is to be asked to Buckingham Palace to have drinks with the royal family. I'm not a huge fan of the monarchy or anything like that. I just think it would be fun to share a drink with the royals in that big old palace.

My friends Paul Newrick and Eric Lanlard have a journalist friend who once got invited to stay overnight at Buckingham Palace and have drinks and dinner with the Windsors. The guy was in such a rush to get there that he threw his clothes and toiletries into a plastic shopping bag and headed to the palace. When he got there, a butler took his bag and ushered him into the parlor, where the entire royal family was waiting for him to have drinks. After drinks, they all went off to change for dinner. When this guy got to his room, he found that the butler had pressed and hung up all his clothes from the bag and then *ironed the bag*! Yes, the butler had perfectly pressed and ironed the disposable grocery bag he had used as a suitcase.

Now, part of me feels like that may have been a bit of a statement from the butler. Or maybe it was standard protocol to tidy up whatever a guest brings into the palace. *Or* maybe the butler was simply having a laugh. Whichever it was, the story made me smile. I guess you could say it gave me a Royal Smile. And now, here's how to make yours!

FILL a cocktail shaker with ice and add the gin, Calvados, lemon juice, simple syrup, and grenadine. Shake and strain into a chilled cocktail glass. Garnish with a lemon twist. Say cheese!

COCKTAIL #82—MAI TAI REVISITED

ORIGINAL TRADER VIC'S 1944 RECIPE

The song—"Do It Again" by the Beach Boys

Do-overs. You don't get very many of those in life. There are things in my life I would have liked to do over:

- The time I crashed my dad's car a week after getting my driver's license because my friend suddenly blurted out, "Turn here!" when we were going through a crowded intersection.
- The time I didn't tell my dad that a woman who was working in his store was stealing from him because I had a crush on her, about which my dad said for days, "My own son cares more about a common criminal than his own father!"
- The time I talked trash about my college roommate for half an hour straight, not realizing he was sitting in the next room hearing every word I was saying.

Crushed ice

1 ounce fresh lime juice (save the lime half after squeezing it)

½ ounce orange Curaçao

¼ ounce orgeat syrup

1 ounce dark rum

1 ounce light rum

Mint sprig

Do-overs would be such a nice way to eliminate those little twinges of old guilt that pop up in the middle of the night or at particularly vulnerable moments.

Which is what makes this drink so special. As you might remember, on page 154 we made a very sweet version of the Mai Tai, which is good though not traditional. But thanks to one of my loyal viewers, I was made aware of the original recipe that became famous at Trader Vic's back in the 1940s. This one is the real deal, complete with a little floating island in the middle! Give it a try and tai one on!

FILL a cocktail shaker with crushed ice and add the lime juice, Curaçao, orgeat syrup, and rums. Shake, pour the liquid along with the ice into a double old fashioned glass, and add enough extra crushed ice to fill to the top. Garnish with an upside-down juiced half lime shell and a mint sprig on top of the ice to make it look like an island. It's one island you won't mind being shipwrecked on!

COCKTAIL #83—GREENBACK COCKTAIL

The song—"Moving on Up" by M People

Ice

1½ ounces gin

1 ounce green crème de menthe

1 ounce fresh lemon juice

Lemon wheel

Did you ever have a friend or acquaintance who had such a big personality they would take over any party or gathering? Or is that you? Do you feel the need to dominate every group of people you hang out with? Are you known for liking to "hold court"? If you do, are you entertaining? Or are you the person everybody tries to escape?

When I was in my teens and twenties, I definitely felt I needed to be the life of the party. I was a struggling comedian and loved the validation of people laughing with me. I saw each gathering of friends as a free audience and did my best to be funny and fun. I always thought people enjoyed my antics, but as time went on, I realized I had no idea if they were just being polite. Nevertheless, I kept on doing it.

One day when I was in my midtwenties my roommate asked if I wanted to go to a party with him. I was tired and not in the greatest mood and remember saying to him, "I can't go; I don't have the energy to entertain everyone." He looked at me like I was nuts and said, "Why can't you just go to the party and enjoy yourself like a normal person?"

After a few moments of feeling insulted, I suddenly realized he was right. I didn't need to go blasting into every event like I was a clown hired to perform at a children's birthday party. I could just go and talk to people. If I wanted to make a joke or got into a fun back-and-forth that inspired me to be funny, then so be it. But I could allow it to happen naturally and enjoy the ebb and flow of the party's vibe. I went to the party and had a nice time and didn't leave feeling exhausted. And never again did I treat a party like a comedy club booking.

What does that have to do with this cocktail? There are some spirits in your bar that are the boozy equivalent of court-holders, liquors with a big personality that can easily dominate and overtake any cocktail they're part of.

Behold, crème de menthe. Much like its friend peppermint schnapps, crème de menthe can blast into any glass or shaker and bulldoze all the other ingredients into submission. Strong mint flavor just doesn't play well with others. If you can teach this crème to simply take it easy in the drink like a normal liqueur, you'll be doing both yourself and the crème de menthe a favor.

The Greenback Cocktail is a drink that does just that. Beware of overpouring your menthe, however; you may even want to underpour it a bit, starting with between ½ and ¾ ounce instead of jumping right to a full ounce. But if you really love mint, then go for it. This drink isn't shy, and you shouldn't be either. Just be ready to have the minty life of the party in your glass. Good luck!

FILL a cocktail shaker with ice and add the gin, crème de menthe, and lemon juice. Shake and strain into an old fashioned glass filled with fresh ice. Garnish with a lemon wheel. Minty fresh!

COCKTAIL #84—THE FUNKSICLE

ANOTHER PAUL FEIG ORIGINAL

The song—"Banana" by Conkarah, featuring Shaggy (DJ FLe–Minisiren remix)

Ice

1 ounce Grand Marnier

1 ounce crème de banane

1 ounce heavy cream or whole milk

By now you know that I love my cream cocktails and also love inventing drinks. Those two passions collide in one glass with the Funksicle! My goal was to make a drink that tastes like a Creamsicle, and to that end, I failed miserably. But I did create a tasty dessert drink that's a little boozy, a little fruity, and a whole lot of delicious. Or so says me.

The Grand Marnier brings the orange but also the sharper booziness of the brandy that is part of the Grand Marnier formula. The crème de banane brings the banana, obviously, and the cream helps to soften and thicken it all up. The first time I made this drink, I used nonfat Lactaid milk and it was too thin and didn't tamp down the extreme personality of the Grand Marnier. But once I switched to heavy cream, the balance was right.

If you want to keep things a bit lighter and use milk instead of cream, stay away from nonfat. Whole milk would be the best bet if your arteries and colon can take it. But whatever you do, I hope you like it. Because it's named after me, your old Drunk Funcle!

FILL a cocktail shaker with ice and add the rest of the ingredients. Shake and strain into an old fashioned glass filled with fresh ice. Funk it up!

COCKTAIL #85—PISCO SOUR

The song—"Olé" by Zoviet

I was lucky enough to go to Peru a few years back and really fell in love with the place. The people were lovely, the scenery was fantastic, and the coca leaves were plentiful. They were everywhere—in bowls at the entrances to stores, in hotel lobbies, in restaurants, in train stations. The locals chewed them all the time because it apparently helps combat altitude sickness in that mountainous country.

Here's the thing—I'm not a drug guy. I never have been. When I was about twelve, my dad and I were looking through an old *National Geographic* magazine; my dad collected them because he loved anything that had to do with nature. (He used to make us watch *Mutual of Omaha's Wild Kingdom,* hosted by a guy named Marlin Perkins. Every Sunday night we had to sit at our small dining room table and watch cute small animals get chased down and eaten by lions and tigers while we ate supper. My dad would always wax poetic and say, "Look at that, the circle of life. Isn't it beautiful?" I didn't agree, since I hated watching some jungle cat lunch on the entrails of a formerly adorable gazelle. Call me crazy.)

The night we were looking through the magazine we came across an antidrug ad showing a staged picture of a "hippie" shooting up heroin with a hypodermic needle. My dad pointed at the picture and said in his scariest voice possible, "You see that idiot? He's wasting his life." My dad then proceeded to go on a fifteen-minute antidrug rant that was so awful and harrowing I vowed right then and there to never ever take drugs lest I have to sit through another one of those lectures. And I never did.

Oh, sure, I tried to smoke pot a few times like everyone else. But whenever I'd take a few hits of that demon weed, it always made me insanely paranoid and then I would be convinced FBI agents were lurking in the bushes. Drugs made no sense to me because I couldn't understand what they did. How did they affect your brain? How could you know if you took too much? I simply didn't want to potentially be that out of control.

Booze I understand. I know how it works on your brain and I know when it takes effect and I know how long it takes to wear off. It's no better for you than some drugs, yet I never worried that after a few martinis I'd wake up days later in jail after having gone on some kind of freak-out spree. No, drugs were not for me.

But in Peru, chewing coca leaves and drinking coca tea just meant that you wouldn't get the splitting headaches and fatigue that come with altitude sickness. While there I drank coca tea constantly, which tasted a lot like green tea, and I took these organic capsules that contained ground-up coca leaves every morning. They didn't get me high, but they definitely kept me from getting sick. I made it through the whole trip feeling great and managed to avoid taking the pills that my doctor had prescribed. If I can stay away from all things medication, I'm thrilled.

But the "medicine" I did discover on that trip was the Pisco Sour. Pisco is more or less a Peruvian brandy made of fermented grape juice. It's somewhere between grappa and cachaça. On its own, it's pretty strong and not necessarily that pleasant. But when it's a part of a Pisco Sour, it's one of the most delicious drinks I've ever had. Tipsy, my friends Paul and Eric, and I drank Pisco Sours all the way across Peru. We took a train most of the way and even brought tuxedoes and formal wear for dinner, though everyone else on the train was wearing shorts and T-shirts to the dining car. But hey, if you can't have a little glamour on a train, where can you?

Anyway, give this drink a try. It's another of the dreaded egg-white cocktails (see page 91), but again, the cocktail is just way better with it included. I'm not a doctor, so I can't say for sure, but I have a hard time imagining there are any germs that could survive a bath in pisco. So crack an egg and send your taste buds (and your liver) to Peru!

Ice

2 ounces pisco

1 ounce fresh lime juice

½ ounce simple syrup (page 112)

1 egg white

Angostura bitters

FILL a cocktail shaker with ice and add the pisco, lime juice, simple syrup, and egg white. Shake vigorously for about 30 seconds to ensure a foamy head, then strain into a chilled Nick and Nora or cocktail glass. Garnish with three drops of bitters on the foam. Go, go, pisco!

COCKTAIL #86—ANGEL'S DELIGHT

The song—"Boogie Nights" by Heatwave

Ice

¼ ounce gin

¼ ounce Cointreau orange liqueur or triple sec

1 ounce heavy cream or whole milk

2 to 3 dashes of grenadine

As you know, I like pink, and that includes pink creamy drinks. Some people think they look like Pepto-Bismol, and sometimes they do. But they're *not* Pepto-Bismol, so what's the problem?

People have hang-ups about a lot of weird things. I always thought the rule that you can't wear white before Memorial Day or after Labor Day was weird. Why *can't* you wear white any time you want if you're okay with footing the cleaning bills? Rules about subjective things like this are made to be broken.

People often say things are rules when they're simply opinions, and sometimes those rules are meant to keep you down. One time when I was an actor I got an offer to audition to be the host of an MTV game show. I was excited about it, but a lot of fellow actors told me that if I got that job I'd never have an acting career because Hollywood would only see me as a presenter from then on. And so I turned down the audition. A little later, Greg Kinnear, who'd hosted *Talk Soup* on E!, got a big acting job in a Jack Nicholson movie, and he was later nominated for an Oscar. I said to the people who told me not to audition to be a game show host, "Greg Kinnear was a TV presenter, and now he's up for an Oscar." To which they said, "Oh, well, *he* was able to do it. But you probably couldn't have."

That's when I decided there are no rules when it comes to subjective things. Everyone's experiences are different because every person is different.

So screw the rules and what people think, and make as many pink drinks as you like! For starters, here's one that's pretty darn delightful. If you really like pink, you can up the amount of grenadine from a few dashes to ¼ ounce or even more. It's up to you!

FILL a cocktail shaker with ice and add the rest of the ingredients. Shake and strain into a chilled cocktail glass. One sip and you'll hear the angels sing!

COCKTAIL #87—ROBIN'S NEST

The song—"Rockin' Robin" by Bobby Day

Ice

1 ounce vodka

1 ounce cranberry juice

½ ounce white crème de cacao

It's another pink drink! And it doesn't have any dairy in it! But it still tastes like ice cream! Why am I so excited?! Because I am!

You wouldn't think the cranberry juice and crème de cacao would work together, but they do. In my business, I'm constantly finding out things that I didn't think would work end up working out great. I didn't think the scene at the beginning of *Bridesmaids* where Annie and Lillian take the workout class in the park for free would get a laugh, so we didn't even put it in the movie until one of our very last test screenings, where it got huge laughs. We weren't sure if the infamous dress shop scene would work, either, and it completely tore the house down in our first test screening.

Life is the same way. You can use your past experience and the expertise of others to try to predict if something will work or not, but you never really know. And so I always say, trying something and having it not work out is always better than not trying it and never knowing if you might have been right.

When I'm making my movies, if someone has an idea for a new line or joke or a different way to play something, even if it sounds crazy to me, I'll usually shoot it if I can. Even when we shoot it and I think it didn't work, I'll often find out in the editing room later that it worked amazingly well. If I hadn't shot it, it wouldn't exist. If I did shoot it but didn't use it, I still learned something.

So give new things a shot—like mixing cranberry juice and crème de cacao. It works, I swear!

FILL a cocktail shaker with ice and add the rest of the ingredients. Shake and strain into a chilled cocktail glass. You can thank me later!

COCKTAIL #88—GOLDEN DREAM

The song—"Dancing Lasha Tumbai" by Verka Serduchka

Ice

¾ ounce Cointreau orange liqueur

¾ ounce Galliano herbal liqueur

¾ ounce fresh orange juice

¾ ounce heavy cream

This dessert cocktail is everything I wanted the Funksicle (page 218) to be. It tastes like a cross between an Orange Julius (remember those?) and a melted Creamsicle (Tipsy's description). And it is delicious. *And* it has my friend Galliano in it. Perhaps you remember this herbal liqueur from the Harvey Wallbanger (page 130), although it was only used as a float on top of that drink.

When I was a teen my friend Ann Lipinski had a bottle of Galliano in her house that sat in the window over the kitchen sink. I was obsessed because I'd never seen a bottle like it before. It looked like a rocket but was filled with delightfully yellowish-gold liquid. One day when her mom wasn't home, Ann asked me if I wanted to taste it. I eagerly said yes and poured a sip. It was a very unexpected taste, like somebody had taken Good & Plenty candy and Good & Fruity candy and melted them down together. (I'm sure the fine folks at Galliano would be thrilled with this very juvenile description of their very fine product.)

I was never a fan of the licorice taste of Good & Plentys; those black, pink, and white candies looked like they would taste fun but assaulted your tongue with bitterness. But I loved Good & Fruitys, and somehow the combo of the two tastes mellowed the licorice through sweetness. So I fell in love with Galliano immediately—but I didn't encounter another bottle for more than forty years.

It was a big moment when I was finally reunited with a bottle of Galliano for my cocktail show. I ordered it from Drizly, and when it arrived at the house, it was like running into an old friend. The bottle now sits proudly on my bar, standing above all the others like the lookout tower outside the Resistance Headquarters in the original *Star Wars*. Even though you may not use this liqueur often, I highly recommend having a bottle of it on your bar, too, if only as a conversation starter. And the conversation will kick into high gear when you make your guests a Golden Dream Cocktail. It's good! Plenty good!

FILL a cocktail shaker with ice and add the rest of the ingredients. Shake and strain into a chilled cocktail glass. Dream on!

COCKTAIL #89—CHARLIE CHAPLIN

The song—"Badtameez Dil" by Benny Dayal and Shefali Alvares

Ice

1 ounce sloe gin

1 ounce apricot brandy

1 ounce fresh lemon juice

Lemon twist

My dad was a master joke teller. He could hold a table of people rapt as he told a joke with great dramatic skill. They were never concise jokes, but they always kept you entertained all the way to the punchline. Dad liked very smart comedy and hated anything that he deemed too "silly."

My mom was the exact opposite. She loved very silly humor. She liked doing funny voices and singing nonsense songs and doing goofy dances. She wanted everything to be light and fun, and she hated when things got too serious or when people started complaining. She was the original "girls just wanna have fun" girl.

I inherited both my parents' sense of humor. I love smart, wordy comedy like my raconteur father favored, and I love really silly comedy as much as my mom did. I'm obsessed with physical comedy and have never been afraid to put a fart joke into a movie or TV show. It's what we call "high and low" in the biz. I love classy comedy but am always ready to undercut it by doing something very low-class, which you already know if you've seen *Bridesmaids*.

I was drawn to this cocktail when I saw it in *Mr. Boston* because of the name—not only because I'm a huge Charlie Chaplin fan, but also because my mother used to tell a story about some big party she attended when she was young where they asked people to perform a talent, and she apparently did an imitation of Charlie Chaplin's Little Tramp walking that brought the house down.

It's a very good drink that tastes a little like fruit punch but in a really good way that's not too sweet. If you've never had sloe gin, this drink is the perfect way to experiment with it. It's gin with sloe berries soaked in it for a long time, and it's an English tradition to put it into flasks in the winter to warm up with when you're out skeet shooting or hiking through the woods. Needless to say, it's very tasty on its own.

So wiggle your mustache, spin your cane, do a funny walk, and mix yourself up a Charlie Chaplin cocktail. My mom would approve!

FILL a cocktail shaker with ice and add the sloe gin, brandy, and lemon juice. Shake and strain into either an old fashioned glass with fresh ice or a chilled cocktail glass. Garnish with a lemon twist. Cheers to Charlie!

COCKTAIL #90—GODCHILD COCKTAIL

The song—"Andiamo a Comandare" by Guerrazzi, featuring Fabietto

Ice

1 ounce amaretto

1 ounce vodka

1 ounce heavy cream

Tipsy and I have no kids, but we do have some wonderful godchildren, whom we love more than life. They are all smart, talented, warm, and kind people who make us proud every day. And so in honor of them and of all the godchildren and godparents out there, here's a delicious recipe for an amaretto-based drink that I know you'll love. Yes, it once again has heavy cream in it! But shouldn't your godfather buy you ice cream when he takes you out for the day?

FILL a cocktail shaker with ice and add the rest of the ingredients. Shake until very cold and strain into a chilled cocktail glass. God, child, it's good!

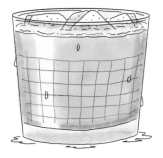

COCKTAIL #91—ESPRESSO MARTINI

The song—"Le Responsable" by Jacques Dutronc

Remember when you were a kid and you wanted something cool and your parents would get you the less cool version of it? Like if you wanted Oreo cookies and they got you Hydrox instead? Or you wanted a pair of Levi's and they got you Wranglers? Or you asked for Heinz Ketchup and you got Hunt's? I know it sounds very bourgeoise to complain about getting anything, since our parents were always fighting to make ends meet and do the right thing for us ungrateful kids.

But, still . . . Hydrox? Boo.

This is the same way I felt about the whole martini craze that swept the nation a number of years ago. I would go to a nice bar and the server would bring us the "martini menu," which was basically just a bunch of crazy mixed drinks served in martini glasses. The idea that pouring any liquid into a martini glass makes it an actual martini is the equivalent of calling a pig on a leash a dog. No, martinis are martinis, and that means it's gin or vodka with some vermouth and a garnish. Case closed.

However . . .

For this drink I'll make an exception to the rule. Why? Because it's really good, it's fairly simple, and it's just rather fun. Once I tried to make it with gin, but it got in the way too much. Stick with vodka for this one. Also, make sure you use fresh, hot espresso that you brew right before you make the drink. Hot coffee that's gone cold on its own is just limp and muddy.

So take advantage of my martini hypocrisy and make yourself this crowd-pleasing cocktail. In other words, espresso yourself! (Wow, you can tell we're getting to the end of the book with jokes like that.)

Ice

1½ ounces vodka

1 ounce fresh, hot espresso

⅔ ounce coffee liqueur (like Kahlúa)

3 coffee beans (optional)

FILL a cocktail shaker with ice and add the vodka, espresso, and coffee liqueur. Shake and strain into a chilled cocktail glass. If you like, garnish by dropping three coffee beans onto the surface of the drink. Go, Java Joe!

COCKTAIL #92—LUCKY FOR YOU!

The song—"Blister in the Sun" by Nouvelle Vague

3 fresh Thai basil
leaves, plus more
for garnish

6 fresh mint
leaves, plus a sprig
for garnish

Slice of fresh
jalapeño

Half a lime, plus
a lime wheel for
garnish

1½ ounces Acre
Mezcal or any
other mezcal

2 ounces passion
fruit juice

½ ounce agave
syrup

Ice

Orchid or
edible flowers
(optional)

I always pretend that I don't want presents, but I love to get them. I also love to give them. There's just something really nice about giving things to each other. It doesn't have to be something expensive or fancy; in many ways, it's nicest when it's not. The best presents are little things that are big on meaning—gifts that show you are paying attention, such as a beloved book, a nice candle in someone's favorite scent, a meaningful trinket . . . or a cocktail.

This recipe was sent to Tipsy and me, along with all the ingredients, by a couple of loyal viewers of our cocktail show, Heidi Haddad and Caroline Somers. It contains so many ingredients I love that it instantly became one of my favorite drinks. I have a real passion for passion fruit (sorry), and I also love very spicy food. The blend of flavors in this drink works so well, you're going to want another one the second you finish the first.

Some of the ingredients can be a bit hard to find, like passion fruit juice and Thai basil, but it's worth the effort to seek them out. So scour the stores, get out your muddler, and make this drink. It'll be lucky for you if you do!

MUDDLE the basil, mint, jalapeño, and lime in a shaker. Add the mezcal, passion fruit juice, agave syrup, and ice. Shake and strain into a Tom Collins glass filled with fresh ice. Garnish with the lime wheel, mint sprig, and basil leaves. You can also add an orchid or edible flowers if you want to get really fancy. Lucky you!

COCKTAIL #93—BLOOD AND SAND

The song—"7 Heures du Matin" by Jacqueline Taïeb

I've never liked my last name. Whenever people try to pronounce it, they get it catastrophically wrong. It should technically be pronounced "F-eye-g," and that's how all the other Feigs out there in the world seem to say it, but not my family—we pronounce it "Feeg." I personally like "Feeg" better than "F-eye-g," but since no one knows to pronounce it "Feeg," I'd rather it was a different name altogether, no shade intended on my ancestors.

When I was a teenager, I created an alter ego for myself named Skylar Billings. I would write scripts about Skylar Billings, a guy with my exact personality and physical appearance but with a much-easier-to-pronounce name. I got the Skylar part from my dad, who once told a story about how one of his cousins almost named one of their kids Skylar and how grateful the kid was not to be stuck with that name. But I thought Skylar sounded like the coolest name of all time.

I don't mind the name Paul, which my parents picked partly for Biblical reasons and partly because they didn't want me to have a name that could be shortened into a nickname, like Robert and Bob or Edward and Eddie. My dad's name was Sanford, always shortened to Sandy, and he didn't like that. Like my mom's name, Elaine, Paul wasn't as prone to getting a nickname unless someone calls me Pauly, which I don't really enjoy. (From time to time, someone will call me "the Feigster," to which I would like to say here in writing: Please don't ever call me that. Please.)

Where the name Billings came from, I have no idea, but I thought it rolled off the tongue and sounded kind of cool. I may be Paul Feig to the world, but in my heart I'll always be Skylar Billings.

Ice

1 ounce scotch whisky

1 ounce fresh orange juice

¾ ounce cherry liqueur (preferably Cherry Heering)

¾ ounce sweet vermouth (preferably Punt e Mes)

1 teaspoon fresh lemon juice

Cocktail cherry

So, what's in a name? Well, this drink is named after an old silent movie starring Rudolph Valentino. I think it's an incredibly weird name for a drink, since it contains the two things I'd like the least in my cocktail glass. But it does sound kind of badass, which is probably why it's stuck for more than a century. Does the Blood and Sand wish it was called something else? Maybe I'll start calling it the Skylar Billings Cocktail.

Whatever the name, it's quite a delicious drink. So call it what you want, but definitely call it into your glass!

FILL a cocktail shaker with ice and add the scotch, orange juice, cherry liqueur, vermouth, and lemon juice. Shake and strain into a chilled cocktail glass. Garnish with a cherry. You won't be silent about this silent movie star!

COCKTAIL #94—THE ROSE

The song—"Spy Party" by Verka Serduchka

Ice

2 ounces dry vermouth

1 ounce kirschwasser (cherry brandy)

1 teaspoon raspberry syrup

Cocktail cherry

I'm so old I remember when you could order a glass of tomato juice as an appetizer at a fancy restaurant. I'm not sure when tomato juice fell out of style as a first course, but I'm all for bringing it back. That or doing a ketchup shooter, which I don't believe exists but which I may now have to invent.

How you start a meal is always important. If you just dive right into your main course without any prelude, you'll get what you need out of the meal, which is sustenance, but you won't be having the full experience. For me, a great meal always starts with an apéritif. As you can predict, my usual opener is a martini, but sometimes I don't want something that strong, especially if I know there are going to be a few different bottles of wine with the meal.

Years ago, Tipsy and I went to a nice French restaurant and they brought us a couple of complimentary apéritifs, basically vermouth with a hint of extra secret ingredients. I had never had vermouth as a drink before, thinking it was only something you used as a minor ingredient in a stronger cocktail. But the vermouth apéritif was really nice. A few years later, my friend David Rosoff opened a Spanish restaurant with a vermouth bar that served many different varieties. They were all delicious and really opened my eyes to vermouth as a standalone player.

So I present to you the Rose, a vermouth cocktail with a bit of cherry brandy and a splash of raspberry syrup. It's a very light drink and a wonderful way to start a meal. Mix up a Rose for your next dinner party and ease your friends into a fantastic evening!

FILL a cocktail shaker with ice and add the vermouth, kirschwasser, and raspberry syrup. Shake and strain into a chilled cocktail glass. Drop in a cherry to garnish. Raise a rose tonight!

COCKTAIL #95—THE EDISON

The song—"Angst in my Pants" by Sparks

I became a professional standup comedian in my twenties, but I'd first tried my hand at it back in Detroit when I was fifteen. I used to have my parents take me to the downtown comedy clubs, since the clubs were bars and I was way underage. But the bouncers let me in because my folks were with me, and because they no doubt thought it was hilarious that a nerdy fifteen-year-old wanted to do standup comedy in front of a bunch of drunk people.

The first gigs I did were at a biker bar called the Delta Lady. They had an open-mic night and I wanted to try my hand at it, having listened to and studied comedy albums my whole life up to that point. I knew how to get laughs in school and figured I'd kill it on an actual comedy club stage. I did my act and got a lot of laughs that at the time I thought meant my act was good. But if you listen to the tape from back then (and yes, there's a tape), it's very clear the audience was laughing *at* me. They had good right to. My act was terrible, a weird mishmash of jokes inspired by Johnny Carson, George Carlin, and Steve Martin. But I caught the standup bug and vowed to do it for a living.

I performed several times after that but was pretty stuck at my freshman-year level of humor. It wasn't until several years later when I moved out to Los Angeles that I actually worked at being a good standup. There were a lot of comedy clubs in LA back then, and they all had open-mic nights. I was able to go out every single night to three or four clubs and do my act at all of them. I did this nonstop for six months, seven nights a week, until I had honed my act to a place where I knew it worked. It was only about fifteen minutes long, but that was all I needed at that point.

One night I went to a club in downtown LA called the Variety Arts Club, and things became real for me. The nightclub had been set up in the basement of this large building that was dedicated to show business. There was an old supper club up on the top floor where they did big variety shows with name performers, and all the offices in the building seemed to be showbiz related, housing talent agents and entertainment attorneys and all the other fringe people that make up both the good and bad sides of the business. I went on that first night and had a great set in front of a packed audience. Because of this, Patty Harris, the woman who booked and ran the club, told me I could become a regular performer there on the weekends.

To become a regular at a club was a huge deal back then. I performed there every weekend for years and met other performers who became some of my best friends. When the club finally closed years later, it was one of the saddest days of my life. The supper club upstairs had been turned into a rather skeevy nightclub, and the comedy club downstairs was used as a holding area for partiers waiting to get into the club. Needless to say, the last thing that crowd wanted to see was standup comedy. After a couple of disastrous weekends, the club closed and we all went our separate ways. I transitioned into acting and writing and stopped doing standup soon after that.

But because of my years at the club, I grew to love downtown LA. It's recently gone through a revival as a bustling metropolis after several decades of decline. Because of this, some great bars have popped up all over the downtown area, and one of the best is the Edison, in a renovated old Con Edison power plant. The recipe below comes from that bar, which should be pretty obvious because of the name. But it's a really great drink, as long as you can procure a bottle of Belle de Brillet, a delicious pear liqueur made from pears and Cognac.

So switch on the power and shake yourself up an Edison. It'll give you a jolt!

Ice

1½ ounces bourbon

¾ ounce fresh lemon juice

½ ounce Belle de Brillet pear liqueur

½ ounce honey

Orange twist

FILL a cocktail shaker with ice and add the bourbon, lemon juice, Belle de Brillet, and honey. Shake and strain into a chilled cocktail glass. Garnish with an orange twist. Make the Edison your medicine!

COCKTAIL #96—THE GARDENER COCKTAIL

The song—"Rose Tinted" by Prefekt

I've never enjoyed gardening. We had a garden when I was a kid, and it was always exciting to see things start to grow and even more exciting when whatever you were growing was ready to be picked. To see a pumpkin appear from a seed that you planted months earlier was pretty cool. But I didn't like to eat anything that had pumpkin in it, and I didn't like actually working in the garden, with all the worms and weeds. So I didn't get much out of the experience.

The problem is I've just never been into nature. I don't like dirt or mud or camping or anything that's too far from a nice clean modern toilet. I've been camping a few times, but it was always like torture for me. I hated when I was in the Boy Scouts and we'd go off for a weekend at some campground. It was always either freezing cold or hot and humid, and we had to use outhouses, which were the equivalent to me of sitting over the gaping mouth of Hell. And eventually someone would throw me into a freezing river or lake and I'd get attacked by mosquitoes and bees and sunburned all over and have to mentally escape into a vision of myself in a tuxedo walking down the street in a cosmopolitan city on my way to some sophisticated event where nature couldn't get me.

So I guess you can say I'm a city boy. I appreciate the *idea* of nature and find reading Thoreau's *Walden* to be a lovely and enlightening experience, but I'll still take sidewalks and skyscrapers over the great outdoors any day.

1 fresh jalapeño, seeded and sliced

1-inch ginger knob, peeled and thinly sliced

¼ cup chopped fresh cilantro

2 ounces fresh lime juice

4 ounces honey syrup (page 108)

4 ounces gin

Ice

MAKES 2 COCKTAILS

However, as has become abundantly clear from this book, I will never turn down a great cocktail, no matter what it's called. The Gardener Cocktail is one of them. It's a spicy, earthy drink that almost feels guilt-free because of its fresh taste. If you're one of those people to whom cilantro tastes like soap, you can always leave it out, or maybe substitute Italian parsley, just to keep the fresh garden taste that muddling herbs brings to this drink.

So roll up your sleeves and get your hands dirty with this very crisp and clean cocktail!

MUDDLE the jalapeño, ginger, and cilantro in a cocktail shaker, then add the lime juice, honey syrup, and gin. Add ice and shake well. Strain into a Tom Collins glasses filled with fresh ice. This is one harvest you won't mind working!

COCKTAIL #97—DODGE SPECIAL

The song—"Come to Me" by France Joli

Ice

1 ounce gin

1 ounce Cointreau orange liqueur

2 dashes of grape juice (white or purple—up to you!)

This drink has a lot of meaning to Tipsy and me. Two of our best friends are Peter and Pam Harper, who live in London. Peter is one of the world's top cancer doctors, and Pam is a brilliant and creative businesswoman who has run companies from Burberry to Halcyon Days. We met them back in 2000 on a Christmas holiday in Scotland. We were staying at a manor house and they were there with their three children and Pam's mother, who was affectionately known as Dodge. We had the best time with them and really fell in love with Dodge. She was eighty at the time and was one of the most fun and lovely people we had ever met.

Dodge was a strong, independent woman who lived on her own all the way up until she turned one hundred. In honor of her centennial birthday, I found this drink that bore her name, and we dedicated our show that day to her. We were supposed to have been in London for a big birthday party for her, but it had been canceled because of the pandemic. So Dodge never got the big blowout she deserved, and sadly, she passed away one month later.

Always upbeat, positive, and fiercely independent, Dodge inspired us to live life to the fullest, whatever age we are. Mix yourself up a Dodge Special and raise it to Dodge and all the other strong, independent women in our lives!

FILL a cocktail shaker with ice and add the rest of the ingredients. Shake and strain into a chilled cocktail glass. Love you and miss you, Dodge!

COCKTAIL #98—THE AVENUE

The song—"Dream Soda" by Televisor

Ice

1 ounce bourbon

1 ounce Calvados apple brandy

1 ounce passion fruit juice

Dash of pomegranate grenadine

Dash of orange flower water

I love New York City, but as a kid growing up in Michigan, I was afraid of it. I'd seen enough movies that made it look dangerous and unappealing. All the jokes about New York when I was a kid were about getting mugged on some seedy side street, so I just assumed you were a goner the minute you stepped foot into NYC.

But in 1982, I went on a trip to New York with a couple of friends of mine, Claire and Rose. We were all in the local repertory theater doing musicals and wanted to see some Broadway shows. In the run-up to the trip, I was scared out of my mind but didn't want to look like a chicken, so I kept my fear secret and focused on the idea of sitting in a Broadway theater and watching the spectacle of the live stage.

However, as soon as we got to New York I fell in love with it. It wasn't the terrifying place I had been led to believe. Sure, you had to keep your wits about you and not get too complacent, but that was also part of the excitement. It was an energy like I'd never experienced before. So many different types of people and so much culture—it was very different from the Detroit suburbs where I was born and raised. I had worked in Hollywood the previous summer as a tour guide and, even though I liked LA, it wasn't the city I thought it would be because it was so sprawling and not really walkable.

But New York was everything. And on that trip I vowed to become a part of it.

I ended up attending film school at the University of Southern California, which was a great experience but which also grounded me in Los Angeles. I wanted to be in the movie business, and LA was where you needed to be. But I never lost my desire to be a part of New York. So when I was hired to direct a few episodes of the Showtime series *Nurse Jackie*, which shot there, I jumped at the chance. I got to live in a hotel right in the heart of Midtown and felt like a real New Yorker.

I decided to buy an apartment there and found a lovely little place on East Fortieth Street between Second and Third Avenues. I was getting more and more television directing jobs in New York, and it seemed like the perfect investment, since I'd be living there so much. And the second I closed the deal on the apartment and got it all set up . . .

. . . I never got another job in New York. I started directing more movies, like *Bridesmaids* and *The Heat* and *Spy*, none of which shot in NYC. I would often stay in my Midtown apartment when I was in writing mode, and I wrote and rewrote several of my movie scripts there. After *Ghostbusters*, I finally signed on to a movie that was going to shoot in the city, mostly because I was dying to work there. Since we were going to be living there for so long during production, Tipsy and I decided to get a slightly bigger apartment. We found an amazing place on the Upper East Side and sold the old place. And then the movie fell apart! So I still haven't made any movies in New York. Yet.

Our new apartment is right between Madison and Park Avenues. So, in honor of my beautiful place, which is currently sitting empty as I continue to strategize how to make a movie in New York so I can finally live there full-time, I present to you the Avenue cocktail. There's a lot going on in this drink, just like there's always a lot going on in New York City. And just like NYC, this drink isn't for everybody. It's got some challenging flavors in it, and they're all competing for your attention. But for those who can handle it, the rewards are great. It'll make you feel like king of the hill, top of the heap!

FILL a cocktail shaker with ice and add the rest of the ingredients. Shake and strain into a chilled cocktail glass. Take a stroll down this Avenue!

COCKTAIL #99—THE LOST LAKE'S FOG CUTTER

The song—"A Far l'Amore Comincia Tu" by Raffaella Carrà

Crushed ice

1 ounce gin

1 ounce aged rum

1 ounce Cognac

2 ounces fresh lime juice

1 ounce orgeat syrup

½ ounce dry sherry

½ ounce orange Curaçao

½ ounce simple syrup (page 112)

Dash of Angostura bitters

MAKES 2 COCKTAILS

We all work hard, don't we? We try to do the right thing day after day, to be good people, to do good things, to cause no harm, to try to make the world a better place. And we're usually so busy doing all this that we don't truly get time to take care of ourselves, to give ourselves a break from the stress and fatigue that come from trying to be productive members of society. So when do we get a chance to unwind?

That's what vacations were invented for. Tipsy and I are very much about vacations. Whether they're far afield, like going to Europe, or a nice weekend away with friends, we realize the importance of giving yourself a break from time to time. It recharges you and gives you a chance to sort out and focus on what's most important in life. You usually come back from vacation with a much clearer head, having had a chance to extract yourself from the forest and really be able to stand back and take in all the trees.

Oh, occasionally it doesn't work out the way it's supposed to. When my *Ghostbusters* movie came out, we'd planned a trip to Capri for the week after the movie opened in theaters. I'd been doing nonstop press ever since we finished post-production, which was quite a marathon, and by the time opening weekend rolled around, I was pretty exhausted. But then the movie didn't do as well as it should have opening weekend. On Monday, we headed off to Italy on what was supposed to be a celebratory vacation. But as I sat next to the pool each day and watched our box office numbers dropping, I realized that the movie wasn't going to make its money back. And it's never a good thing when your movie loses money at the box office.

The vacation became even more stressful as I tried to force myself to relax while watching the movie I'd worked so hard on for so long sink into the mud. I found myself swinging between irritation and manic celebration as I pretended things were fine. I came home from vacation almost more exhausted than when I'd left.

So what should we do if the serenity of a great vacation is out of reach, because of finances or schedules or responsibilities or just our state of mind? Or if we simply can't even go on vacation? I believe the answer is to simply find and create moments that *feel* like a vacation. It can be as small as going out to get your favorite treat or as big as throwing a party for your closest friends to have some drinks and commiserate about what everyone's going through at the moment. Even the smallest breaks can be a form of vacation.

If you want a cocktail that feels like a mini-vacation, then have I got a recipe for you. This drink is a day off in a glass. It's a trip to the tropics. It's a deep breath of fresh air on a sunny beach. Sure, it's absolutely loaded with booze, and so it should be handled with care. But it's also delicious and sure to lift your spirits as you lift these spirits.

So mix yourself up a Lost Lake's Fog Cutter. Your stress will never know what hit it!

FILL a cocktail shaker with crushed ice and add the remaining ingredients. Shake hard to break down the ice so that it's almost slushy. Divide the mixture into two tiki mugs or old fashioned glasses and add more crushed ice to fill. Garnish with a cocktail umbrella or whatever other fun item you can find. After all, it's your vacation!

COCKTAIL #100—THE CORPSE REVIVER #2 *OR* THE FUNCLE 100

The song—"Amapola" by Xavier Cugat

Ice

1 ounce gin

1 ounce Cointreau orange liqueur

1 ounce Lillet Blanc apéritif

1 ounce fresh lemon juice

1 to 3 drops absinthe or pastis

Cocktail cherry

We did our final daily *Quarantine Cocktail Time!* episode on June 27, 2020. While we continued to do shows once every week or two after that, this was the end of our daily run. We never took a single day off during the first 100 episodes.

We did a new episode every evening at 5 p.m. PST, come rain or shine, good mood or bad. It was one of the most fun and wonderful times of my life. The circumstances that put us all in that situation were horrendous. A worldwide pandemic was taking the lives of so many people and wreaking havoc on every nation's economy. And then thrown into the middle of that were heartbreaking incidents of racial inequality and violence, as well as a mindboggling backlash to all the measures that the science and medical communities asked us to take to curb the coronavirus. It was all too much to bear.

But to be able to meet so many wonderful new people online through our show, and to be able to raise money for charities and make people aware of organizations they might not have known about before—it all helped Tipsy Faunt and me feel like we had at least a modicum of control over a completely out-of-control situation.

And we got to make a lot of drinks.

The Corpse Reviver #2 is an old drink that's famous as a hangover remedy. It's definitely from the "hair of the dog" school, which says you fight a hangover with more booze. While I don't personally subscribe to that theory, some people do swear by it.

For me, this drink stands for an antidote to all that we had been through in those terrible months when the virus first took off and we had very little clue how strong it was and if it was even possible to fight it. We were all consumed with fear, and yet, for a month or two, that fear bonded us together. Everyone in the world was vulnerable to this unknown killer. For that short amount of time, before the backlash began and the finger-pointing started to overtake our lives and our politics, we were united in our concern for one another. And that was a lovely thing.

So mix up this elixir and raise a toast to everyone on this planet. We're truly all in this together.

FILL a cocktail shaker with ice and add the gin, Cointreau, Lillet Blanc, lemon juice, and absinthe or pastis. Shake and strain into a chilled cocktail glass. Drop in the cherry and revive yourself!

THE FUNCLE 100
(JUST BECAUSE I HAD TO MAKE THIS FINAL DRINK MY OWN!)

Make the Corpse Reviver #2 the exact same way but add two dashes of orange bitters before shaking. *Vive la différence!*

BUT WAIT—THERE ARE MORE PAUL FEIG ORIGINAL RECIPES!

JUST WHEN YOU THOUGHT I'D RUN OUT . . .

Here are a few more Paul Feig originals that I've created for various events and occasions. I'm Paul Feig, and I approve these drinks.

THE MICHIGAN BON BON

Ice

2 ounces fresh, hot espresso (regular or decaf)

1 ounce dark crème de cacao

½ ounce Cherry Heering or other cherry liqueur

1½ ounces heavy cream

Ground cinnamon

I created this drink for a fundraiser in honor of a great congresswoman from my home state of Michigan, Elissa Slotkin. In Michigan, we're known for our cherries, and I wanted this to taste like a nice chocolate-covered cherry bon bon. And guess what? It does! It has now become one of Tipsy's and my favorite drinks.

Break out the heavy cream, folks. It's another lactose-intolerant nightmare/dream from your good old Drunk Funcle!

FILL a cocktail shaker with ice and add the espresso, crème de cacao, Cherry Heering, and heavy cream. Shake vigorously and strain into a chilled cocktail glass. Top with ground cinnamon. *Très bon bon!*

THE RAKE/THE RAKEFRESHER

My favorite magazine in the world is *The Rake*, a style magazine dedicated to timeless men's fashion. Over the years, I've become friends with Wei Koh, the magazine's founder and president, and Tom Chamberlin, its editor in chief. They've done a few articles about me over the years, but in the summer of 2020, they actually put me on the cover.

I'd never been on the cover of a magazine because, well, what magazine in their right mind would put me on the cover? However, Wei and Tom are such lovely gentlemen and were so supportive of my *Quarantine Cocktail Time!* show that they wanted to feature me. So to help pay them back for this unpaybackable gift they gave me, I invented two cocktails just for them and their readers.

And now I'm sharing them with you! Isn't that just the kind of thing a cover boy would do?

THE RAKE COCKTAIL

Ice
1 ounce gin
½ ounce Dubonnet Rouge apéritif

¼ ounce Cherry Heering or cherry liqueur
¼ ounce Cointreau orange liqueur
Juice of ¼ lime

FILL a cocktail shaker with ice and add the rest of the ingredients. Shake and strain into a chilled cocktail glass. Dress up and drink it down!

THE RAKEFRESHER

Ice
1 ounce gin
1 ounce dry vermouth

1 ounce Cointreau orange liqueur
Club soda
Orange twist

FILL an old fashioned glass with ice and add the gin, vermouth, and Cointreau. Stir, then top with club soda to taste (add more for a not-so-sweet drink, less for a sweeter concoction). Garnish with an orange twist. Fresh!

THE TWO ENDS OF THE POOL:

THE SHALLOW END/THE DEEP END

As you already know, I love my blue drinks. One night we had a small pool party for a couple of friends and I decided to invent a drink for the occasion. What came out of it were these two drinks, which are honestly just spins on a classic Cosmo. But the fun is in how blue you want to make them. The more blue Curaçao you add, the more orange taste and sweetness you get. So it's totally up to you.

    I highly suggest finding some fun drink ornaments to hang off the lip of the glass for these cocktails. They're both fun drinks, so they might as well look the part. Why the heck not? Dive in!

THE SHALLOW END

Ice

1½ ounces Artingstall's Brilliant London Dry Gin

1 ounce Cointreau orange liqueur

½ ounce fresh lime juice

2 dashes of blue Curaçao

Lime wheel or slice

FILL a cocktail shaker with ice and add the gin, Cointreau, lime juice, and Curaçao. Shake and strain into a chilled cocktail glass. Garnish with a lime wheel or slice. Swimmingly good!

THE DEEP END

FOLLOWING the recipe above, use ½ ounce blue Curaçao instead of 2 dashes. Call the lifeguard!

THE OTHER SPACE

Ice

¾ ounce gin

¾ ounce Midori melon liqueur

¾ ounce blue Curaçao

¾ ounce Cherry Heering or other cherry liqueur

1 to 2 dashes of raspberry syrup

Cocktail cherry

In 2015 I produced a sci-fi comedy show called *Other Space*. It was a real passion project for me, something I had created years earlier when I had a deal at NBC. They had liked the script but didn't have any place for it on their schedule. So it went into my files as something I loved but sadly couldn't get made. About ten years after that, I was contacted by executives at Yahoo! who were looking to produce three TV series for a new streaming service they were launching called Yahoo! Screen. I immediately pulled out *Other Space* and said I had the perfect show for them. They loved the script and we hired writers and a cast and made eight episodes. I was so happy with how it all came out. We worked incredibly hard on the series, and I was certain it would be a hit in the sci-fi community.

Sadly, Yahoo! Screen didn't catch on with the public. And so *Other Space*, along with the other two series, crashed and burned. It was devastating to me because I knew the show was good. The cast was so funny and talented, and our writers came up with amazing material for them. Alas, nobody ever saw it.

But five years later, in 2020, the eight episodes were picked back up by a sci-fi service called Dust and have found their audience. I will forever be grateful to them for giving our show another chance. While I was promoting the relaunch of my beloved series, I invented a cocktail in honor of the show. Since the series takes place in a colorful alternate universe, I wanted the drink to reflect that visually.

This drink is as fun to make as it is to taste, so take your time preparing it. I'll warn you right now, though, it's a sweet one. But isn't it the sweetest feeling when something you love gets a second chance?

FILL a clear mixing glass with ice and pour in the gin, then the Midori, then the Curaçao, then the Cherry Heering. Take time to enjoy watching the colors blend into one another. Stir until very cold, then strain into a chilled cocktail glass or coupe. Pour the raspberry syrup in and let it settle at the bottom of the glass. Drop in a cherry, either on its own or on a cocktail pick. Hold the glass up to the light to enjoy the colors, then drink. It's out of this world!

ANOTHER OTHER SPACE

IF the Other Space is too sweet for your taste, make the same recipe but pour the drink into a Tom Collins glass over ice cubes and top with club soda. It'll still send you into orbit!

ZOEY'S EXTRAORDINARY COCKTAIL

Ice

1 ounce Artingstall's Brilliant London Dry Gin

½ ounce Cherry Heering or other cherry liqueur

4 ounces blood orange juice

Blood orange slice

Cocktail cherry

I was lucky enough to be an executive producer on the Emmy-winning NBC show *Zoey's Extraordinary Playlist*, a musical dramedy about a young woman who's in an MRI machine when an earthquake hits and ends up with every song ever recorded downloaded into her brain, and she then sees and hears them reflecting people's innermost thoughts. It's a very funny and emotional show with an amazing cast, headed up by the great Jane Levy and created by the supremely talented Austin Winsberg. Our first season did very well and was quite beloved, so we were rewarded with a season two. For the premiere of that second season, I invented this drink.

I used blood orange juice because music runs through Zoey's veins. You know, like blood! Then of course I had to use some of my beloved Cherry Heering, because, well, it's really good—and also the color of blood! Yikes, it's starting to sound like *Zoey's* is a horror show. It's not. It's delightful, and so is this drink. So mix one up and stream a few episodes of *Zoey's Extraordinary Playlist*!

FILL a cocktail shaker with ice and add the gin, cherry liqueur, and blood orange juice. Shake and strain into an old fashioned glass over fresh ice. Garnish with a blood orange slice and cocktail cherry. It'll have you singing in the streets!

THE LOVE LIFE

Ice

3 ounces
Artingstall's
Brilliant London
Dry Gin

1 large dash
raspberry syrup

3 drops cherry
bitters

Cocktail cherry

Another show I executive produce is *Love Life* on HBO Max, in which each season follows one character's quest for love. The first season starred my wonderful pal Anna Kendrick, and the second season starred the fantastic William Jackson Harper. We had a big premiere in New York City for the second season of the show, and I invented this drink for us to serve at the after-party.

The interesting thing about creating a cocktail is watching someone else prepare it. I had taken great pains to make sure this drink was very subtle so it wouldn't get too sweet or too bitter. Basically, I wanted it to be both a bit sweet *and* a bit bitter . . . just like love. Clever, huh? Well, imagine my surprise when I watched the bartender dump a much bigger pour of raspberry syrup and some very hearty dashes of bitters into the mixing tin and then shake the drinks like he was trying to kill a rat inside the shaker. It was quite eye-opening.

But you know what? When he poured me the drink, it was actually really good. Super-cold, sweeter than I had wanted it, but also nicely balanced with the bitters.

The moral of this story? This is a drink you can sort of make into anything you want. If you want it sweeter, do a big dash of syrup. Less sweet? A smaller one. And your bitters drops can either be big or small, depending on how hard you shake the bitters bottle over the drink. I guess you could say that this cocktail is just like love in another way—it never turns out quite the way you expected it to, but it's usually still pretty great. Love it up!

FILL a cocktail shaker with ice and add the gin, raspberry syrup, and bitters. Shake until cold and strain into a chilled cocktail glass. Garnish with a cocktail cherry. To life! *Love Life*!

THE EMILIA-TINI

Ice

1½ ounces
Artingstall's
Brilliant London
Dry Gin

¼ ounce vodka

½ ounce Lillet Rose
apéritif

Lemon twist

In 2019, I made a Christmas-themed romantic comedy called *Last Christmas*, which was inspired by the music of the late, great George Michael. It was written by my friend Emma Thompson, actor/writer extraordinaire and all-around amazing person, who sent the script to me out of the blue one day. I immediately fell in love with it and committed to direct and produce it.

It had a great central role at its heart that could be a real showpiece for the right actor. I had met with Emilia Clarke several years earlier in what we call in the biz a "general meeting," meaning you sit down with someone without any specific job or role in mind and just get to know them. I had really fallen for Emilia at that first meeting because I simply didn't expect her to be so funny. I only knew her as the Mother of Dragons from *Game of Thrones* and expected her to be as serious in real life as her character was on the show.

So imagine my surprise when this incredibly funny and fun person sat down before me. We talked and laughed for an hour, and as soon as she left, I said to my producing partner at the time, Jessie Henderson, that we had to put Emilia in a comedy. The minute I read Emma's script, I knew the main character was the perfect role for Emilia. She would get to be funny, but we also needed an amazing actor to pull off all the emotions and drama that the story put her character through.

Well, Emilia completely nailed it, was an absolute delight to work with, and is now a very good friend. So I jumped at the chance to do a virtual interview with her for the Edinburgh TV Festival in 2020. The festival wondered if I would make a drink with Emilia at the top of the interview, so I invented the Emilia-tini. This is just a variation on a Vesper Martini, but

I gave it an Emilia twist by pulling back a bit on the gin and vodka and adding Lillet Rose, one of her favorite drinks.

And here it is: the Mother of Cocktails for the Mother of Dragons. Three cheers for one of the nicest people on the planet, Emilia Clarke!

FILL a mixing glass with ice and add the gin, vodka, and Lillet Rose. Stir until very cold, then pour into a chilled martini glass. Squeeze a lemon twist over the surface of the drink, rub the lip of the glass with the twist, and drop it into the drink. I tini, you tini, we all tini for the Emilia-tini!

THE *BRIDESMAIDS* COCKTAILS

Yes, I directed *Bridesmaids*. I'm very proud of the film and am thrilled with its enduring popularity. It was a great script written by Kristen Wiig and Annie Mumolo and featured one of the most talented casts of all time. We had tons of fun making it, and it ended up doing very well at the box office. And it definitely saved my career.

I had made *Freaks and Geeks* ten years earlier, and while things had gone well overall in my TV career, my movie career was in the toilet. *I Am David*, the movie I made right after *Freaks and Geeks*, had bombed horribly. I followed that up with a family Christmas film called *Unaccompanied Minors* that had also cratered at the box office. So I was firmly in what is known in the industry as movie jail, which basically means no one else is going to let you make another movie.

It was very depressing because all I've ever wanted to do in life is make movies. When you realize that you're never going to be allowed to follow your dreams again, it's a bitter pill to swallow. I was very lucky to be working on several great TV series, like *The Office*, *Arrested Development*, and *Nurse Jackie*, while also directing episodes of *Mad Men*, *30 Rock*, and others. But all I really wanted to do was make movies.

So when I got a call out of the blue from my agent that a wedding comedy script I had attended the reading of several years earlier was going to get made and that my friend Judd Apatow wanted me to direct it, I was thrilled. I met with Kristen to make sure she wanted me to do it, too, and she was kind enough to agree. And the rest is history.

Nine years after the film came out, I did a watch-along event over Zoom to raise money for a great charity called Family Promise (which supports families experiencing homelessness), as well as in honor of all the people who had to cancel their wedding plans because of the COVID quarantine. I created three drinks for the event, which we made during breaks in the watch-along. They are all *Bridesmaids*-themed drinks, and if you're a fan of the movie, you'll understand what each is in reference to.

Beyond that, I just think they're really good drinks. But you be the judge. Mix up one or all of these—and hold on for one more day!

CAKE BABY SPRITZ

Ice
1½ ounces gin

1 ounce cranberry juice
Club soda

FILL a wineglass with ice and add the gin and cranberry juice. Top with club soda. Let them drink cake!

FRITZ BERNAISE (AKA SHITTIN' IN THE STREET)

Ice
1 ounce gin
1 ounce Midori melon liqueur

1 ounce fresh lime juice
Cocktail cherry

FILL a cocktail shaker with ice and add the gin, Midori, and lime juice. Shake until cold, then strain into a chilled cocktail glass. Drop in a cherry. Drink away!

JORDAN ALMOND

1½ ounces amaretto
1 ounce gin
½ ounce pure maple syrup (or honey or agave syrup)

1 ounce heavy cream
Ice

POUR the amaretto, gin, and maple syrup into an empty cocktail shaker. Stir until the syrup is dissolved. Add the heavy cream and ice to the shaker and shake vigorously until the drink is very cold. Strain into a chilled cocktail glass. It's happening!

THE MATT NEWMAN

Ice

2 ounces blended scotch whisky

½ ounce Amer Picon apéritif

½ ounce Bénédictine herbal liqueur

1 teaspoon maraschino cherry liqueur

2 dashes of cherry bitters

Cocktail cherry, with a little bit of syrup from the jar

Champagne is an interesting drink because it has so many different connotations to so many different people. In the United States we tend to think of Champagne as something we only drink when we're celebrating milestones and victories. But back when Laurie and I started dating, we took a trip to London, where Laurie had a lot of friends. We would go visit them and every one of them would open a bottle of Champagne when we arrived as a "welcome to our house" beverage. It blew my mind because to me, you opened Champagne only if it was your anniversary or New Year's Eve.

I think this casual European view of Champagne is the right way to go. It's not like you have to open a five-hundred-dollar bottle of Dom when guests come over. You can get great sparkling wine and more reasonable Champagne for not much more than a mid-level bottle of wine. But the minute your guests hear a cork pop, they will appreciate the gesture and marvel at how cool you are.

So is this cocktail Champagne-based? No! I just went off on another tangent about booze. I sort of can't help it. But I created this recipe for my friend Matt Newman, who took Tipsy and me on a champagne tour in France a few years ago. I wanted to name something special after him. So I now present to you a very delicious, almost cola-like drink called the Matt Newman. Confused? Just make one and it'll all make sense!

FILL an old fashioned glass with ice and add the scotch, Amer Picon, Bénédictine, maraschino liqueur, and bitters. Stir to combine, then drop the cherry on top and stir in the extra syrup that collects in your barspoon when you scoop the cherry out of the jar. Toss one back for Matt!

OLLIE'S THORN

Ice

2 ounces gold
añejo tequila

1 ounce Kahlúa or
any other coffee
liqueur

4 dashes
Angostura cocoa
bitters

4 dashes cherry
bitters

Cocktail cherry

My friends Paul and Eric are very involved in an amazing organization called the Back Up Trust, which helps people with spinal cord injuries. Every year they have a fundraising dinner at a big, fancy ballroom and everyone shows up in black-tie and gowns and bids on all kinds of donated items in both a silent auction and a traditional "I've got five hundred, do I hear a six hundred?" type auction. The most recent year I attended, a young man named Ollie Thorn, who was paralyzed in a motorcycle accident, was acting as a presenter during the auction. He was such a lovely fellow and had such an amazing attitude about life that in addition to donating money to Back Up, I also wanted to create a drink that was as nice yet as strong as Ollie is.

Hence, Ollie's Thorn. (Clever, huh?) Truth be told, this is my variation on a drink called a Brave Bull, which is usually made with tequila blanco and Kahlúa. But I wanted this to be a bit richer in spirit, much like Ollie himself, and so used gold añejo tequila instead. I also added one of my new favorite ingredients, Angostura cocoa bitters, which really elevates any drink that has a mocha bend to it. And then, since I'm still a kid from Michigan at heart, I couldn't resist adding a few dashes of cherry bitters to round it all out. The result is a drink that's quite delicious to either begin an evening with or serve as an apéritif to send it into the history books in fine, tasty fashion.

And so I now present to you Ollie's Thorn. It's one thorn you won't mind getting stuck by!

FILL an old fashioned glass with ice and add the tequila, Kahlúa, and bitters. Stir until combined and garnish with a cocktail cherry. Hooray for Ollie!

IF YOU'RE EVER IN HUNGARY AND WANT A MUCH STRONGER DRINK . . .

THE last time I was in Budapest, I discovered that the fine folks at Zwack, the company that produces Unicum, an extremely strong herbal liqueur that will knock you on your ass much the same way Jäger will, had put out a coffee-flavored version of their drink called Unicum Barista. As of this printing, it's only available in Hungary, but I'm sure it will make its way out into the world soon. It's quite delicious and quite strong. So, if you're in the mood for a rocket-fuel version of Ollie's Thorn and can find a bottle, substitute the Unicum Barista for the Kahlúa. It's like a mocha missile in a glass. Kaboom!

THE HOLIDAY COCKTAILS

Ice

1½ ounces gin

1 ounce passion fruit liqueur

½ ounce Aperol aperitivo

Dash of crème de cassis black currant liqueur

Dash of raspberry syrup

VALENTINE'S DAY: I'M GIN LOVE!

Remember Valentine's Day in grade school when everybody would give one another those little Valentine cards? For me, it was always a gauge of whether there was anyone in my class who might have a crush on me. I would look forward to it for days, certain that I was about to receive a secret message from my future wife. But I usually either came up empty or would get some courtesy cards from a few of the nicer girls in class with some sort of "Please don't think I'm attracted to you" message written on it like "To a very funny guy!" or "Thanks for the laughs!" As much as I hoped I'd get some proclamation of undying love, I always walked away at the end of the day feeling like Valentine's Day had been created by popular people to make unpopular people feel bad about themselves.

I'll be honest. Tipsy and I never celebrate Valentine's Day. We made a vow when we first met that every day should be a potential Valentine's Day in its own way, meaning we would just surprise each other from time to time with something nice that showed our love. And so we do that to this day. Little gifts, surprise date nights, or just an unexpected favorite food treat—we like to keep the romance alive by being unpredictable instead of waiting for the officially mandated Day of Love.

But that said, I do still get her something on Valentine's Day because . . . well . . . better safe than sorry. That's how you stay married for thirty years! So, mix up an I'm Gin Love for your loved one and make them feel like they just got the most romantic card in the class!

FILL a cocktail shaker with ice and add all the ingredients. Shake until cold, then strain into a chilled cocktail glass. Raise a glass to the one you love!

HALLOWEEN: THE ECTOPLASM GRIMLET

Most people love Halloween and hate candy corn. Well, guess what? I love them both. So break out the high-fructose corn kernels and make this treat that's definitely not a trick!

Ice

1½ ounces Artingstall's Brilliant London Dry Gin

1 ounce St. Germain elderflower liqueur

½ ounce fresh lime juice

½ ounce Midori melon liqueur

2 pieces of candy corn

FILL a cocktail shaker with ice and add the gin, St. Germain, lime juice, and Midori. Shake and strain into a chilled cocktail glass. Carefully melt the back of one piece of candy corn with a match or kitchen torch. Press the melted side onto the other piece until they are fused together, and then slide them onto the rim of the glass as a garnish. Ooo, scary!

I'm Gin Love!

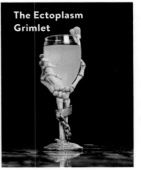

The Ectoplasm Grimlet

Last Christmas

GTFO 2020

THANKSGIVING: THE FAMILY DINNER

I have always loved Thanksgiving, but my mother didn't. She liked it fine when we went to my aunt Sue and uncle Ferd's house, because it meant they would cook and she didn't have to. But she was miserable when she had to host. My dad did his best to help, but his contribution usually ended with taking the turkey in and out of the oven and grinding up chicken livers to make a big liver ball with nuts pressed into the sides, which my grandma and uncle would scoop up with crackers while I tried not to throw up watching them eat it. So Thanksgiving always brought mixed feelings of fun and angst for me, being an only child and very close to my anxiety-filled mother.

Since my parents were Christian Scientists, they didn't drink. But I always felt that if they had, our Thanksgivings would have been much more stress-free, at least when my mother had to cook. And so I invented this Thanksgiving drink in the hopes that someday I'll get a time machine and be able to go back to my childhood and pour my mom a tall one of these before she starts cooking. I hope someday I get the chance, because I miss my mom. Get on it, science!

1 ounce Artingstall's Brilliant London Dry Gin

1 ounce Calvados apple brandy

½ ounce Cherry Heering or other cherry liqueur

½ ounce fresh lemon juice

¼ ounce allspice dram liqueur

¼ ounce pure maple syrup

8 dashes of cranberry bitters

Ice

Fresh or frozen cranberries

POUR the gin, apple brandy, cherry liqueur, lemon juice, allspice dram, maple syrup, and cranberry bitters into a cocktail shaker and stir until the maple syrup is dissolved. Add ice and shake. Pour the drink and ice into a highball or Tom Collins glass. Add more ice to fill and garnish with fresh or frozen cranberries. You're welcome!

CHRISTMAS: LAST CHRISTMAS

Who likes mint? Who likes chocolate? Who likes booze? Well, if you like all three, here's the ultimate Christmas gift from your old friend Funcle Claus!

Hey, here's a fun fact: The term *Santa Claus* comes from the turn of the twentieth century when Spanish journalists in the United States would say the name "Saint Nicholas," but because of their heavy accents, it sounded like they were saying "Sant Nick-clous." And so the American journalists made fun of them and started saying "What did you say? Santa Claus?" So, yes, the name Santa Claus came from people making fun of other people's accents. Whee! Ugh.

And on that dark note, here's a minty chocolatey boozy concoction that no one will make fun of!

Ice

1 ounce Artingstall's Brilliant London Dry Gin (or vodka, if you must)

1 ounce light crème de cacao

½ ounce crème de menthe

Candy cane stick

FILL a cocktail shaker with ice and add the gin, crème de cacao, and crème de menthe. Shake and strain into a chilled martini or Nick and Nora glass. Add a candy cane stick and serve. Naughty *and* nice!

NEW YEAR'S EVE: GTFO 2020

I created this drink in honor of 2020, a true shit show of a year. There was only one way to usher it out properly—with a big sloppy bucket of booze! However, this booze bucket is really quite tasty. And dangerously innocent tasting. So watch out!

Ice

½ ounce Artingstall's Brilliant London Dry Gin

½ ounce vodka

½ ounce mezcal

½ ounce pisco

½ ounce peach schnapps

½ ounce Aperol aperitivo

2 dashes of Parfait Amour liqueur

2 dashes of peach bitters

1 ounce club soda

Orange slice

FILL a cocktail shaker with ice and add the gin, vodka, mezcal, pisco, peach schnapps, Aperol, Parfait Amour, and bitters. Shake and pour into an old fashioned glass over fresh ice. Top with club soda and garnish with an orange slice. Drink until you forget how terrible 2020 was.

BUT WAIT! THERE'S EVEN MORE!!!

RECIPES FROM
MY WONDERFUL
CELEBRITY FRIENDS!

Sure, I hit up some of my famous friends for their favorite cocktails. Wouldn't you?

ANGELA KINSEY!

THE KINSEY GIN FIZZ

2 ounces gin

1 ounce lemon juice

½ ounce pure maple syrup

1 egg white

Ice

Club soda

Lemon wedge

I had the absolute honor of directing nineteen episodes of the U.S. version *The Office* over the course of many seasons. Every day on that set with those actors and writers was a joy. It was there that I first met Angela Kinsey. She played a very uptight character, but in real life she is nothing but fun. I had the distinct honor of getting to hide from the cameras the fact that she was eight months pregnant when I directed the now-famous "Dinner Party" episode. A combination of flower bouquets, throw pillows, and close-ups were able to mask her delicate condition. And we laughed about it the entire time. Angela is a delight.

When I first sent Angela a bottle of my gin, our mailbox store guy who handles all of Tipsy's and my shipping, and who is also very generous with the various holistic herbal remedies he sells in his store, sent Angela and her husband, Josh, a box filled with ginger honey crystals and herbal hand sanitizer but forgot to include the gin. So, after me going on and on to Angela about how great my Artingstall's gin is, she opened the box and thought that maybe she had misheard me and that I had my own brand of ginger.

Fortunately, I was able to have the actual bottle sent to her. Angela and Josh made the below drink with my gin, and it's mighty delicious. I love that they used maple syrup, which is fast becoming one of my favorite cocktail ingredients. Mix up a fizz and don't forget the gin!

POUR the gin, lemon juice, maple syrup, and egg white into an empty cocktail shaker and shake vigorously for 15 seconds. Add ice to the shaker and shake another 15 seconds, until cold. Strain into a highball glass filled with fresh ice, top with club soda, and garnish with a lemon wedge. Gin for the win, Angela and Josh!

JENNA FISCHER!

THE JENNALEE

Ice

2 ounces vodka

4 ounces fresh grapefruit juice

Splash of cranberry juice

Club soda

Grapefruit slice

Cranberries

It was through *The Office* that I also got to know Jenna Fischer. Another of my favorite people in the business, Jenna is a truly wonderful person who was an absolute joy to work with.

Here's an unknown fact about one of Jenna's scenes. I directed Steve Carell's final episode, "Goodbye, Michael," and in it is a scene where Jenna's character, Pam, decides to take a break from work to sneak out and see a movie. I was in post-production on *Bridesmaids* at the time, and Greg Daniels very kindly suggested that it should be the movie that Pam is going to see. I was very flattered until we both realized that Ellie Kemper, a regular on the show, was also in my movie. We knew there was a chance that when we shot the scene in front of the theater, we would see the poster for the film, and it seemed just too meta for Pam to be going to see a movie starring someone who worked in her office. Plus, I worried that if *Bridesmaids* bombed it would look too weird for Pam to be going to see it. So in the episode, Pam goes to see *The King's Speech*. Oh well. At least it won some Oscars.

Jenna was kind enough to send me this recipe, which she and her husband, Lee, love. It's basically a modified Greyhound, but their addition of cranberry juice and club soda makes it come alive in a way that a normal Greyhound doesn't. It's refreshing and fun, and I know you're going to like it. It's Pam-tastic!

FILL a Tom Collins or highball glass with ice and add the vodka, grapefruit juice, and cranberry juice. Stir to combine and top with club soda. Stir again and garnish with a slice of grapefruit and a couple of cranberries. Jennalee-licious!

HENRY GOLDING!

HENRY'S HONEY PLUM G&T

2 hachimitsu umeboshi (sweet honey-soaked pickled plums)

1 teaspoon honey or pure maple syrup

Ice

2 ounces gin

1 ounce umeshu (sweet plum liqueur)

4 ounces tonic water

Henry Golding is the nicest man in the world. He's kind, patient, funny, fun, and a great friend. He's also an amazing actor. I worked with Henry for the first time on my film *A Simple Favor* and we had so much fun together, both on and off the set. We would meet up for cigars and drinks at his rental house in Toronto once a week to relax and take a break from the sometimes stressful and high-pressure (but ultimately always satisfying) demands of making a movie. We would try a new libation every week and worked our way through several types of whiskeys, wines, and other spirits over the course of making the film. But we never really made any mixed drinks.

So when I asked Henry what his favorite cocktail was for this book, he surprised me with this recipe. It's made with ingredients you may have to conduct a bit of a search to find, but the resulting concoction is well worth your time and effort.

Henry was born in Singapore and raised in London, then moved back to Singapore to host and produce his own travel show before becoming an actor. I really love that this drink brings together his British and Asian sensibilities. So mix one up and have a Golding good time!

COMBINE the plums and honey or maple syrup in a highball glass and muddle with a wooden muddler. Fill the glass with ice and stir in the rest of the ingredients. It's plum good!

MICHELLE YEOH!
THE FIVE YEOH-LARM FIRE

1 fresh jalapeño pepper, seeded and roughly chopped

3 dashes of Tabasco sauce

2 dashes of sriracha

2 ounces tequila blanco

½ ounce Cointreau orange liqueur

1 ounce fresh lime juice

Ice

Cayenne pepper

Margarita salt or coarse kosher salt

Lime wedge

I've been a fan of Michelle's for decades. Tipsy and I love watching Hong Kong films with lots of action, and Michelle Yeoh was always our favorite badass. She makes her fighting skills look effortless and is both disarmingly beautiful and completely deadly. She's also an amazing actor. But before I met her, she seemed like a mythical creature. I mean, how could someone that awesome exist in real life? Then, when I was making *A Simple Favor* in Toronto, Henry Golding called one night and said, "Hey, do you want to have dinner with Michelle Yeoh?"

My head almost exploded. How was it possible that I had the opportunity to not only meet Michelle Yeoh but also share a meal with her? I almost turned down the offer because I was terrified that (a) I might come off like a total idiot fanboy, (b) she might be so cool and above it all that I would simply resort to pummeling her with questions about her films, and (c) she might beat me up. Who knows? She's so tough and cool in her movies maybe that's how she is in real life, too.

Well, the second I showed up at the restaurant, I was greeted by the funniest, most warm and charming person I think I have ever met. Michelle and I immediately connected, and I sat next to her and we talked and laughed and joked and ate and drank and a lifelong friendship began. It was such an honor to have her in my films *Last Christmas* and *The School for Good and Evil* and show the world how funny she is, and we now look for every opportunity to work together on anything and everything.

Michelle loves very spicy food, and so when I asked her for her favorite cocktail, she immediately said a spicy margarita. But not your typical spicy margarita. No, it had to be one that's spicy enough for someone as tough as Michelle. Her secret is muddling not only jalapeños but also hot sauce in the drink. Then, an added blast of cayenne pepper mixed with salt on the rim will leave your lips burning, your tongue on fire, and your brain filled with spicy joy. If you like hot, you'll love this drink from my wonderful badass pal. Prepare to get Yeohed!

MUDDLE the jalapeño, Tabasco, and sriracha in a cocktail shaker until combined. Add the tequila, Cointreau, lime juice, and ice. On a small plate, mix together some cayenne and salt. Use the lime wedge to wet the rim of the glass, and then dip the rim into the salt-cayenne mixture. Add fresh ice to the glass and strain in the drink. Feel the burn!

CHARLIZE THERON!

THE CHARLIZE THERON GIBSON

How awesome is Charlize Theron? I'll tell you, my friend. If you list awesomeness on a scale from one to ten, Charlize is a billion. I first worked with her when I was directing *Arrested Development*. She had a recurring role on the show in its final season (and this was *after* she'd won the Oscar for her amazing performance in *Monster*). Simply put, Charlize loves comedy and wanted to be a part of the funniest show on TV at the time. We had so much fun on the two episodes I did with her, and I even got to have her walk on water across a swimming pool. Just another day at the office!

Charlize and I stayed in touch ever since then and were always looking for another project to work on together. Enter *The School for Good and Evil*. The role of Lady Lesso, the dean of the School for Evil, just seemed like the perfect role for Charlize, one that I knew she could have tons of fun playing. So I was over the

moon when she said she was in. In my business, you have certain people who you know will always bring a great performance and who are also just wonderful people to work with to boot. That is Charlize in a nutshell. We had the best time shooting our movie in Belfast, and I thank my lucky stars every day that she's my friend.

So when I asked her if she had a recipe she wanted to contribute, not only did she give me one but she wrote it up herself. And so now, here in her own words, is her recipe for this truly killer drink. Take it away, Charlize!

Ice

2½ ounces vodka

½ ounce dry vermouth

Frozen cocktail onions
(Yes, I said frozen. As in, put the cocktail onions in the freezer. It's insane but works. Trust me. It's like a nice little ice cube of pickled oniony goodness.)

OKAY, first, get your ingredients ready:

FILL a mixing glass with ice and add the vodka and vermouth, then stir until chilled. Feel free to add more vodka. And vermouth. You've had a long day. Strain into a cocktail glass. Make sure it's a chilled glass. Because you're classy like that.

POP a couple of frozen onions into your drink, prop your feet up, and savor that first sip, 'cause you're drinking a motherfucking Charlize Theron Gibson!

See, I told you she was awesome.

KERRY WASHINGTON!
THE VERY CHERRY KERRY

Ice

5 ounces tart
cherry kombucha

2 ounces fresh
orange juice

½ ounces fresh
lime juice

1 teaspoon honey

Club soda
(optional)

Joining Charlize at a billion on the awesomeness scale is Kerry Washington. I had always been a fan of Kerry's, but it was when I saw her on *Scandal* that I knew she was someone I wanted to work with and become friends with. Since one of my best friends in the world, Betsy Beers, was a producer on the show, I was able to reach out to Kerry and let her know how much I wanted to put her in one of my projects. We tried several times over the years but could never quite find the right one. And then along came *The School for Good and Evil*, or as I like to call it, the gift that keeps on giving. I knew that Kerry could be both hilarious and commanding in the role of Professor Dovey, dean of the School for Good. And she was.

Kerry is one of the sweetest people I know, and when I asked her if she had a drink she wanted to share for the book, she really wanted to do something nonalcoholic. She has a soft spot for kombucha and gave me this truly tasty recipe that's not only good but good for you! Offer this one up to the nondrinkers at your next party, and tell 'em Kerry's got their backs!

FILL a highball glass with ice, add the kombucha, juices, and honey, and stir to dissolve the honey. Top with a bit of club soda to add some extra fizz, if you want. Kerry on with this delicious nonalcoholic treat!

ALLISON JANNEY!

THE JANIKAZI

Ice

2 ounces vodka
or dry gin (like
Artingstall's)

¾ ounce Cointreau
orange liqueur

½ ounce fresh lime
juice

½ ounce fresh
lemon juice

Juice of 1 kumquat

Yes, that's right, this book has cocktail recipes from not just one but *two* Oscar winners! Allison and I had run in the same circles for quite a while, but it wasn't until I made the movie *Spy* that I actually met her and got to work with her. She's a true delight and the absolute life of the party. If you ever throw a shindig and want to make sure it turns into an insanely fun time, invite Allison Janney.

We shot *Spy* in Budapest in the summer of 2014, and on our weekends off, Tipsy would rent the services of a Venetian water taxi that did tours up and down the Danube. On Allison's first weekend with us, a bunch of the cast members, including Miranda Hart, Jessica Chaffin, Katie Dippold, and Sam Richardson, along with Laurie and me, set off down the Danube for a day-long cruise. It turned into an all-day dance party, with Allison bringing out her playlists and deejaying the entire trip, a journey that at one point saw us all dancing on the roof of the boat as it cruised through the beautiful Hungarian countryside. It was truly one of the most special days of my life.

Allison is the best, and she was kind enough to share her twist on a kamikaze shot, which adds more tart fruit flavor and presents it in cocktail form. Why in cocktail form? Because a drink this good is too delicious to shoot. So get out your citrus squeezer and get your juices flowing! It's Janney-rific!

FILL a cocktail shaker with ice and add all the ingredients. Shake and strain into a chilled cocktail glass. It's Oscar-winning good!

STEVE HIGGINS!
THE SOUR STEVE

Ice

Juice of ½ lime

Juice of ¼ lemon

½ ounce
Bénédictine

2 ounces blended
scotch

4 dashes
Angostura bitters

1 dash pure maple
syrup

½ egg white*

Lemon twist

One of my oldest and best friends in showbiz is Steve Higgins. You know him as Jimmy Fallon's sidekick Higgins on *The Tonight Show,* but to me he'll always be the guy I sat with at a late-night Los Angeles diner in the mid-1980s when we were both struggling standups and had the classic angst-filled conversation that begins, "What if we never earn a living in this industry?" Steve went on to run *Saturday Night Live* under Lorne Michaels for more than twenty years and counting and is one of the funniest, smartest, and nicest people in the comedy world. I couldn't love him more.

Steve loves whiskey sours but wanted to put a twist on the standard recipe, so he created this take on an old drink called a Frisco Sour. Steve loves egg white in his sours, which he says brings them a creamy goodness that elevates the drink (and I concur!), so he included that in this recipe. He also added Angostura bitters to counteract the brightness of the citrus juices and then added maple syrup for a bit of hearty sweetness. The result is . . . well . . . just mix yourself up one and see how good it is! (If you're still nervous about using egg whites, Steve wants you to know that the drink is just as good without them.)

So shake one up and step into a Sour Steve! Hey-oh!!!

FILL a cocktail shaker with ice and add the lime and lemon juices, Bénédictine, scotch, bitters, and maple syrup. Shake until cold. (*If you're using an egg white, shake these ingredients plus the egg white vigorously without ice for 30 seconds, then add ice and shake until cold.) Strain into an old fashioned glass over fresh ice and garnish with a lemon twist. How sweet this sour is!

AND NOW—GO FORTH AND COCKTAIL!

It's all up to you now. I've tried to give you some meaningful advice on all things cocktails and the cocktail lifestyle, as well as lots of drinks to make. What you do with it all is your choice. But I do sincerely hope you'll take away one thing from this book, and that is . . .

Whether you drink or not, whether you want your life to be fancy and stylish or whether you want it to be casual and down-to-earth, the bottom line is that life doesn't have to be boring. In fact, it should never be boring. Bored people are boring people, as the saying goes, and I know that none of you are boring. Life is about meeting people, about learning things and passing on experiences, about being interested as well as being interesting, about doing good and making the world a better place than the one you came into, and about always doing the right thing.

Can cocktails help you on this quest?

As far as I'm concerned, they can be a part of it. They can be the social lubricant, the catalyst for gathering together, the fun in the middle of the work, and the spice in the appreciation of life. They can remind you that you're a grown-up with grown-up duties and responsibilities, and they can be the momentary break from those responsibilities.

Cocktails and cocktail culture should be fun, but always be responsible and think about the world and the people around you as much as you think about yourself. This is truly the way to make the most out of adult life.

So go forth and cocktail, my friends. And whenever you can, please raise a glass to your good ol' Funcle and Faunt, Paul and Laurie. Oh, and Buster the Scottie, too. Cheers!

NICE THINGS TO DO WITH YOUR MONEY

Here's a list of the organizations we supported during our *Quarantine Cocktail Time!* show. One of the main reasons I did my show at the beginning of the pandemic, besides wanting to help people have fun while we were all locked in our houses, was to help raise money for various charities. It started out supporting Covid and pandemic relief organizations but then expanded to additional worthy charities that were dealing with some of the other issues raised in that very disruptive year of 2020. I made sure to always vet these charities with either Charity Navigator or through people I knew who were involved with the groups and could vouch for their legitimacy.

If you want to donate to any of these extremely worthy charities, just type any of their names into your web browser and you'll find a link and how you can donate to each of them. Like I always said on my show, if you've got a lot of money, donate a lot; if you've got a little money, donate a little; and if you don't have any extra money to give, contact them and see how you can help with your time and energy. You'll be helping people, you'll feel good about yourself, and you'll earn that cocktail you couldn't wait to make!

A Chance in Life

A New Way of Life

ACLU

Action Against Hunger

Advancement Project

Americares

Anti-Violence Project

Beaumont and Henry Ford Hospitals in Detroit, MI

Black Lives Matter

Black Visions Collective—The George Floyd Memorial Fund

Black Youth Project

Boys and Girls Club of America

Callen-Lorde

CanadaHelps

Careers Through Culinary Arts Program

CDC Foundation

Center for Law and Social Policy

Charity Navigator

Choose Love

Color of Change

CORE, Children of Restaurant Employees

DC Central Kitchen

Doctors Without Borders

DonorsChoose

Dream Defenders

Equal Justice Initiative

Fair Fight

FairShare

Feed the Children

Feeding America

Film2Future

First Book

Fistula Foundation

Forgotten Harvest

Gary Sinise Foundation

GiveDirectly

GiveIndia

Giving Kitchen

HealthWell Foundation

Heart to Heart

Hospitality Action

Howard Brown Health

Institute for Free Speech

International Rescue Committee

Know Your Rights Camp

Lawyers' Committee for Civil Rights Under Law

Local food bank

Los Angeles Regional Food Bank

MATTER

Meals on Wheels

MedShare

Michigan Hospitals

NAACP Empowerment Programs

National Immigration Law Center

No Kid Hungry

Operation Gratitude

Partners in Health

Partnership with Native Americans

Peace Over Violence

People for the American Way

PolicyLink

Post New York Alliance

Preemptive Love

Project C.U.R.E.

Public Justice Center

Royal British Legion

Semper Fi & America's Fund

ShelterBox

Take Action Minnesota

Team Rubicon Disaster Response

The Leadership Conference on Civil and Human Rights Education Fund

The Mankind Initiative

The Minority Corporate Counsel Association

The Okra Project

The Restaurant Workers' Community Foundation

Direct Relief

The Southern Poverty Law Center

The United Way of Buffalo and Erie County

Together Rising

Tony La Russa's Animal Rescue Foundation

UNICEF

Unicorn Riot

Union Rescue Mission

United Way

USBG Bartender Emergency Assistance Program

WIRES

World Central Kitchen

World Health Organization

UNIVERSAL CONVERSION CHART

Measurements should always be level
unless directed otherwise.

⅛ teaspoon = 0.5 mL

¼ teaspoon = 1 mL

½ teaspoon = 2 mL

1 teaspoon = 1 barspoon = 5 mL

1 tablespoon = 3 teaspoons =
3 barspoons = ½ fluid ounce = 15 mL

2 tablespoons = ⅛ cup =
1 fluid ounce = 30 mL

4 tablespoons = ¼ cup =
2 fluid ounces = 60 mL

5⅓ tablespoons = ⅓ cup =
3 fluid ounces = 80 mL

8 tablespoons = ½ cup =
4 fluid ounces =
120 mL

ACKNOWLEDGMENTS

always look at the writing of acknowledgments with dread. Not because I don't like to thank people for the help and support they've given me—but because I'm always certain I'm going to forget someone. On the rare occasion I've won an award, I always dreaded the acceptance speech because I'd inevitably get so nervous that I'd forget to thank people that I definitely should have thanked. Poor Tipsy has been left out of so many acceptance speeches in our more than thirty years together that I have no idea why she's still with me. And so I now face this page with the same trepidation I always do.

That said, like all things in life, I just need to dive in. So, here goes. . . .

I'd first and foremost like to thank the great Cassie Jones, editor extraordinaire, for wanting to publish this book in the first place and for always being available to field neurotic questions ranging from "Is this joke funny or annoying?" to "Does this drawing look like it was done by a five-year-old?" and always staying honest and upbeat in the process. Equal thanks to Jill Zimmerman for wading through all my weirdly constructed sentences and wordings and keeping me from sounding like an idiot while somehow still allowing my oddly juvenile voice to come through. Thanks to my amazing CAA team of Mollie Glick, Abby Walters, Bryan Lourd, Ida Ziniti, Matt Martin, Michael Rosenfeld, and Jacquie Katz for always having my back. Huge love to the visual wizards Liz and Max from Haarala Hamilton Photography in London and Lauren Volo in New York City, as well as props stylist Laura Fowle, for putting up with all my mugging and somehow getting a lot of great pictures in spite of it. Endless appreciation to my favorite watering holes in the world— Dukes Bar, Ralph Lauren Polo Bar, Claridge's Hotel, Il Tinello, and Mark's Club—for letting me behind your spectacular bars to be photographed pretending that I actually know what I'm doing when you all know how to do it so much better. A big cheers to Ted Haigh and Todd Maul for all their boozy inspiration. An astronomical debt of gratitude to Angela Kinsey, Jenna Fischer, Henry Golding, Michelle Yeoh, Charlize Theron, Kerry Washington, Allison Janney, and Steve Higgins for lending their recipes, time, and names to this presumptuous little tome and totally classing up the joint. And to all our loyal Instagram *Quarantine Cocktail Time!* viewers, this book would never have happened if you all didn't take an interest in watching a bartending wannabe stumble through his mixology lessons on a daily basis while we all thought the world was ending. I truly love you all.

On the Artingstall's Brilliant London Dry Gin side (did I mention that I have my own gin brand?), I will never be able to thank Ravinder and Manjit Minhas enough for making my gin dreams come true and seeing potential in a guy whose only qualification to get into the spirits business is that he drinks a lot. You are the best partners a person could ever ask for. Endless thanks to Alex Kotlyar, Tyler McLeod, and Donald MacLellan, who make the machine run to get Artingstall's out into the world and the hands of consumers. Major props to Jordan Goodman and Anuj Sathe for putting me together with Ravinder and Manjit in the first place. The drinks world said an uncool director could never have his own brand of alcohol, and yet somehow you proved them wrong. A big hug to Ian Lamarra, Rosie Nixon, and Bridget Arsenault for constantly spreading the word of Artingstall's. And endless thanks to Cara Tripicchio, Leah Chang, and Darrell Borquez of Shelter PR; Daisy Bell, Sophie Lane, and Katie Tims of BellCo; and Noah Gelbart, Ian White, and Jennifer Karlik of CAA Global Brands for keeping the word out in the streets.

Finally, truckloads of love to all the people in this world who get me through life with their friendship and support: Betsy Beers and Bruce Cormicle, Peter Freedman, Michael Patrick King and Craig Fisse, Marla Garland, Delphine Mann, Paul Newrick and Eric Lanlard, Peter and Pamela Harper, George Culucundis and Trish Wadley, Michael Ostrow and Roger Stoker, Stanley Tucci and Felicity Blunt, Pino and Claire Ragone, Melissa McCarthy and Ben Falcone, my cousins Philip, Laurel, and Leslie and all their kids and partners, Peggy, Howard, Michael, and Katy Pattis, Jim and Ann Gianopulos, Chris Aronson, Daria Cercek, Judd Apatow and Leslie Mann, Rob Watzke and Helen Slater and my goddaughter Hannah,

Wei Koh, Tom Chamberlin, the team at *The Rake*, Gianluca Isaia, Giulia Natale, Mo Coppoletta, Hani Farsi, Anda Rowland and the gang at Anderson & Sheppard, Nick Sullivan, Nick, Alexandra, Max, and Freddie Foulkes, Ahmed and Anouk Rahman, Andy Poupart and Michele Free, Santa and Sebag Montefiore, George and Luna Papageorgiou, Laura Allen Fischer, Brent White, Ian Cunningham, Paul Chandler, Erica Weis, Anna Callin, Teddy Shapiro and Joanna Schwartz, Dan Magnante, Zach Bianco, Zoe Dennis, Jessie Henderson, Renee Kurtz, Mike and Patty Sampson, Lori Sampson and the whole Sampson clan, Paul Chepikian and Terry Mason, Vince and Beth Tornabene, their kids and all the Artingstalls, and anyone else whom I know I've missed. (I told you I was going to screw this up.)

And saving the biggest thanks for last: Major cheers to my legal eagle and close friend Warren Dern, who always has my back; nothing but love to Greg Lubin, the hardest-working man in show biz, for helping endlessly with this book and Artingstall's even though he doesn't drink; undying gratitude to Alessandro Palazzi, without whom I would be nothing in the cocktail world; everything to my long-gone but never forgotten parents, Sanford (who never drank except on the day I was born, according to him) and Elaine (who always wanted to drink but couldn't and so made rum-soaked candy at holidays to do it under the cover of dessert); and to Laurie, my Tipsy, my best friend, the love of my life and spark to my flame, my first, my last, my everything—I will love you until the cows come home and then once they're home I'll send them away so I can keep on loving you more and more. Thank you for more than I could ever list here. You are the gin to my lemon twist, the beautiful glass to my cocktail shaker, the cheers to my toast, and I can never thank you enough for it all.

Oh yeah, and to Buster, who is now an official service dog. What service he provides we still haven't figured out.

INDEX

NOTE: Page references in *italics* indicate photographs.

HarperCollins books may be purchased for educational, business, or sales promotional use. For information, please email the Special Markets Department at SPsales@harpercollins.com.

FIRST EDITION

DESIGNED BY RENATA DE OLIVEIRA

Illustrations by Paul Feig except the following: Tom Kelley Archive/Getty Images: page 38; Lordprice Collection/Alamy Stock Photo: page 45

Geometric pattern by Seamlees Patterns/Shuttersotck

Photographs by Haarala Hamilton except the following: Lauren Volo: pages ii–iii, iv–v, 48, 53, 75, 87, 98, 106, 119, 138, 139, 159, 177, 199, 260, 282, 296; Bettmann/Getty Images: page 9; Jonn Leffmann: page 13; Russell Lee/Getty Images: page 15; MGM/Ronald Grant Archive/Alamy Stock photo: page 16; Universal Television LLC/NBCUniversal: page 22; Old Visuals/Alamy Stock Photo: page 28; Topical Press Agency/Getty Images: page 30; Pictorial Press/Alamy Stock Photo: page 35; Aubrey Hart/Getty Images: page 36; Popperfoto/Getty Images: page 37; Kurt Schraudenbach/Süddeutsche Zeitung Photo/Alamy Stock Photo: page 39; Trinity Mirror/Mirrorpix/Alamy Stock Photo: page 42; H. Armstrong Roberts/Alamy Stock Photo: page 43; Adobe Stock: page 46; Paul Popper/Popperfoto/Getty Images: page 49; Paul Feig: page 89; Alexis Halejian/Redbird: page 145; Yahoo Screen: page 255; Dimitrios Kambouris/Getty Images: pages 259 and 276; Ollie Thorn: page 265; Dan Spineau/Philux Photo with styling by: Tyler McLeod: page 267; Helen Sloane © 2022 Netflix Inc.: page 277

Library of Congress Cataloging-in-Publication Data has been applied for.

ISBN 978-0-06-316069-9

22 23 24 25 26   LSC   10 9 8 7 6 5 4 3 2 1